MICROSOFT OFFICE XP EXAM
REFERENCE POCKET GUIDE

THOMSON

COURSE TECHNOLOGY

Australia • Canada • Mexico • Singapore • Spain • United Kingdom • United States

THOMSON
COURSE TECHNOLOGY ™

Microsoft Office XP Exam Reference Pocket Guide
is published by Course Technology.

Managing Editor:
Nicole Jones Pinard

Product Manager:
Kim Crowley

Editorial Assistant:
Christina Kling Garrett

Production Editor:
Debbie Masi

Contributing Author:
Jennifer Campbell

Composition House:
GEX Publishing Services

QA Manuscript Reviewers:
Nicole Ashton, John Freitas, Jeff Schwartz, Alex White

Book Designer:
GEX Publishing Services

ISBN 0-619-10939-4

Brief Table of Contents

TABLE OF CONTENTS

ABOUT THIS BOOK

HOW TO USE THIS BOOK

The Microsoft Office XP Exam Reference Pocket Guide is a reference tool designed to prepare you for the Microsoft Office User Specialist (MOUS) exams. This book assumes that you already understand the concepts that are the basis for the skills covered in this book, and, therefore, the book can be used as a study companion to brush up on skills before taking the exam, or as a desk reference when using Microsoft Office programs.

The Structure of this Book

There are six chapters in this book. The first chapter in the book, Exam Tips, provides some backgound information on the MOUS Certification program, the general process for taking an exam, and some helpful hints for preparing and successfully passing the exams.

The remaining five chapters each cover a different Office program: Word, Excel, Access, PowerPoint, and Outlook. Each program-specific chapter begins by covering program basics in a brief Getting Started section. This section covers the basic skills that are not specifically covered in the MOUS exams, but that are essential to being able to work in the program. The Getting Started section is followed by the complete set of skills tested by the MOUS Certification exams, starting with the Core or Comprehensive exam, and then followed by the Expert exam where applicable. These sections are labeled and ordered to exactly match the Skill Sets and Skill Activities tested in the MOUS Certification Exam. Clear, bulleted steps are provided for each skill.

Because there are often different ways to complete a task, the book provides multiple methods where appropriate for each skill or activity, including Menu, Button, Keyboard, Mouse, and Task Pane methods. The MOUS exams allow you to perform the skills using any one of these methods, so you can choose the method with which you are most comfortable to complete the task.

Technical Concerns

This book assumes the following regarding your installation of Office XP and your computer's setup:

- ☐ You have installed Office XP using the Typical installation.
- ☐ You have a document open and ready to use when required to work within a specific document. For instance, when you are asked to format a spreadsheet or word processing document, you are given the steps to format in different ways; you must decide which formatting options you will use, and on what section of your document.

☐ You have the correct toolbar(s) open. All toolbars are referenced in this book, and in each Getting Started section there is information about displaying a toolbar if you do not have it open. However, the steps to display a certain toolbar are not repeated for every skill.

☐ You have an Internet connection to complete certain steps, and that you are familiar with how to connect to the Internet.

ACKNOWLEDGEMENTS

Thank you to all of the people who contributed to the process of this book. I specifically want to thank Jason Moore of Ball State University for his insightful reviews, Christen Kunciw, Quality Assurance tester, for testing for accuracy, Debbie Masi for being the production editor, and Kim Crowley, the developmental editor and product manager, for her patience, wisdom, and insight. I also want to thank Mike and Emma for providing me with support, encouragement, and welcome diversions.

Jennifer T. Campbell

Exam Tips

☐ What is MOUS Certification?
☐ Certification benefits
☐ The MOUS Certification process
☐ Choosing an exam
☐ Preparing for the exam
☐ Finding a testing center
☐ Taking the exam
☐ Receiving exam results

What is MOUS Certification?

Certification is a growing IT industry trend whereby a software or hardware company devises and administers exams for users that will demonstrate their abilities to use the software or hardware in an effective manner. By passing a Certification exam, users prove their abilities and knowledge of the software or hardware to prospective employers and colleagues. Microsoft Office User Specialist Certification, or MOUS Certification, is a series of exams used to identify and measure Microsoft Office skills that business professionals and educational institutions recognize and respect. They can confidently use MOUS to assess and measure the computer skills of current and future staff members or students.

The MOUS exams are developed, marketed, and administered by Certipoint, Inc. (formerly Nivo International), a company that has exclusive license from Microsoft. The exams are available in multiple languages and in many countries. Exams must be taken at an authorized MOUS testing center called an iQcenter. In order to become an iQcenter, a facility must have a quiet room with the proper hardware and software, as well as trained personnel to manage the exams.

Certification Benefits

Achieving MOUS Certification in one or several of the Microsoft Office XP programs can be beneficial to you and your current or prospective employer. Certification demonstrates that you have the ability to perform a certain level of skills in the given program. For example, if you have passed the Microsoft Word Core Certification exam and you are interviewing for a job that requires knowledge and use of Word to complete business-related word processing tasks, MOUS Certification in Microsoft Word will indicate to your employer that you have the necessary skills to perform that aspect of the job. It also indicates not only that you have a certain level of skill, but that you also have the initiative to prepare for, sign up for, pay for, and take an exam. MOUS Certification can help you to increase your productivity within your current job and is a great way to enhance your skills without taking courses to obtain a new degree.

THE MOUS CERTIFICATION PROCESS

There are five steps to successfully completing MOUS certification, as outlined in the table below and discussed in the remainder of this introductory chapter.

Table ET-1: MOUS Certification Process

Action	Description
Choose an Exam	Choose from one of the following exams, based on your skills and interests: Word Core Word Expert Excel Core Excel Expert Access Core Access Expert PowerPoint Comprehensive Outlook Core
Prepare for the Exam	Select the method that is appropriate for you, including taking a class or purchasing self-study materials
Find a Testing Center	Find a site close to you using the iQcenter locator on www.microsoft.com/mous, and either make an appointment or verify that the center accepts walk-ins
Take the Exam	Bring payment and a valid picture ID; be sure to read the exam directions before starting the exam
Receive Exam Results	You will find out your results immediately. If you pass, you will receive your certificate two to three weeks after the exam

CHOOSE AN EXAM

The MOUS Certification program offers exams for the five main programs of Microsoft Office XP: Word, Excel, Access, PowerPoint, and Outlook. For Word, Excel, and Access there are two exams available, one covering Core skills and an Expert exam testing the more advanced skills in the program. The Core exam covers basic skills such as formatting and using graphics that will help you demonstrate your proficiency in the application. The Expert exam focuses on more advanced features of the application such as collaborating with other users, working on the Web, and importing data from and exporting data to other programs. The Expert exam assume that you know the Core skills, but the same questions will not be covered on both exams. The PowerPoint and Outlook exams have only one level each, covering both basic and advanced skills. Choose an application and an exam that will help you in your current position or job search, or one that tests skills that match your abilities and interests. You can find the list of skills covered in each exam on the MOUS exam Web site *www.microsoft.com/mous*. You can also find more information on the exams at *www.certcities.com/certs/mous* and at *www.microsoft.com/traincert/mcp/mous*.

About the Office Master Certification

If you are familiar with or could benefit from having knowledge of all of the applications, then your ultimate goal might be to become an Office Master. This is not one exam; rather, you must pass all of the five following exams: Word Expert, Excel Expert, Access Core, PowerPoint Comprehensive, and Outlook Core.

PREPARE FOR THE EXAM

How you choose to prepare for an exam depends on your current skill level, which you can determine by reading through the objectives for the exam. As stated earlier, a list of skills covered in each exam is provided on the official MOUS exam web site *www.microsoft.com/mous*.

Preparing for a Certification exam might be as involved as taking an introductory class and learning the program in its entirety. If you are already familiar with the program, preparation may only entail purchasing study materials and learning on your own all of the skills or those with which you feel you are not as familiar. If you have been using the program on a regular basis, you may need simply to review the skills on the objectives list for the exam you choose and brush up on those few that are problem areas for you.

Take a Class

Preparing for the exam by enrolling in a class on the program is a good option if you are a complete beginner, or if you know the basics but you want to take an advanced class to prepare for an Expert exam. The benefits of taking a class include having an instructor as a resource, having the support of your classmates, and receiving study materials such as a lab book. Some classes are even geared specifically towards taking and passing a certification exam, and are taught by instructors who have passed the exam themselves. Your local community college, career education center, or community/continuing education programs will most likely offer such courses. Classes range from one day to several weeks in duration. You could also take a distance learning class from an online university or through one of the local options listed above; distance learning offers the flexibility of learning from home on your own time, but teaches the same skills as a traditional classroom course.

Purchase Materials for Self-Study

You can prepare on your own to take an exam by purchasing materials at your local bookstore or online. To ensure that the study materials you are purchasing are well-suited to your goal of passing certification, you should consider the following: favorable reviews (reviews are often available when purchasing online); a table of contents that covers the skills you want to master; and the MOUS seal. The MOUS seal indicates that Microsoft has confirmed that the publisher accurately covers all of the skills for a particular MOUS exam, provides testing material on these skills, and Microsoft recognizes the book as being an adequate tool for Certification preparation. Because the book you are reading now is designed as a reference guide and does not contain material testing the reader's knowledge of the skills, it does not have the MOUS seal. Depending on your abilities, you might want to purchase a book that will teach you the skills and concepts step-by-step and then test your knowledge. If you are only in need of a refresher, this book is all that you need.

Here is a list of suggested products published by Course Technology that you can use for self-study. You can purchase these books online at *www.course.com*.

☐ **Certification Circle Series:** The Certification Circle Series enables students to focus on the skills that will appear on the Microsoft Office User Specialist (MOUS) exams. The books in the series are available alone or packaged with **SAM, Skills Assessment Manager for Microsoft Office XP**, which is a powerful Office XP assessment and reporting tool that will help you test and measure your proficiency in individual programs and skills. SAM Study Guides are mapped by page number to the Certification Circle texts, which means you can take a SAM exam, determine the exam results, and then refer to the exact page in the corresponding Certification Circle text for help on any given skill. The series includes the following titles bundled with SAM XP:

For Core Exam preparation:

Microsoft Access 2002 – MOUS Core and SAM XP

Microsoft Excel 2002 - MOUS Core and SAM XP

Microsoft Word 2002 – MOUS Core and SAM XP

Microsoft Outlook 2002- MOUS Core and SAM XP

For Expert/Comprehensive Exam preparation:

Microsoft Access 2002 – MOUS Expert and SAM XP

Microsoft Excel 2002 – MOUS Expert and SAM XP

Microsoft Word 2002 – MOUS Expert and SAM XP

Microsoft Office XP – MOUS Master

Microsoft PowerPoint 2002 – MOUS Comprehensive and SAM XP

☐ **New Perspectives Series:** For detailed information on this Course Technology book series, visit (*www.course.com/newperspectives/*)

For Core Exam preparation:

New Perspectives on Microsoft Access 2002 Introduction

New Perspectives on Microsoft Excel 2002 Introduction

New Perspectives on Microsoft Outlook 2002 Brief

New Perspectives on Microsoft Word 2002 Introduction

For Expert/Comprehensive Exam preparation:

New Perspectives on Microsoft Access 2002 Comprehensive

New Perspectives on Microsoft Excel 2002 Comprehensive

New Perspectives on Microsoft Outlook 2002 Introduction
New Perspectives on Microsoft PowerPoint 2002 Comprehensive
New Perspectives on Microsoft Word 2002 Comprehensive

☐ **Shelly Cashman Series:** For detailed information on this Course Technology book series, visit (*www.scseries.com*)

For Core Exam Preparation:
Microsoft Office XP Introductory Concepts and Techniques
Microsoft Office XP Advanced Concepts and Techniques
Microsoft Access 2002 Complete Concepts and Techniques
Microsoft Excel 2002 Complete Concepts and Techniques
Microsoft Word 2002 Complete Concepts and Techniques

For Expert/Comprehensive Exam Preparation:
Microsoft Office XP Introductory Concepts and Techniques
Microsoft Office XP Advanced Concepts and Techniques
Microsoft Office XP Post-Advanced Concepts and Techniques
Microsoft Access 2002 Comprehensive Concepts and Techniques
Microsoft Excel 2002 Expert Comprehensive Concepts and Techniques
Microsoft PowerPoint 2002 Comprehensive Concepts and Techniques
Microsoft Word 2002 Expert Comprehensive Concepts and Techniques

☐ **TOM, Training Online Manager for Microsoft Office XP:**
TOM is Course Technology's MOUS-approved training tool for Microsoft Office XP. Available via the World Wide Web and CD-ROM, TOM allows students to learn Office XP concepts and skills actively and realistically through both guided and self-directed simulated instruction.

FIND A TESTING CENTER

As stated above, you must sign up to take MOUS certification exams at an authorized testing center, called an iQcenter. iQcenters are often located in educational institutions, corporate training centers, and even some computer stores.

You can find a listing of iQcenters in your area by logging onto *www.microsoft.com/mous*. Once you locate a center near you, you will need to call the iQcenter and schedule a time to take the exam or find a center that allows walk-in exams.

Exams are offered in multiple languages and in several countries, although each site might not offer all languages. If you require a specific language, you should check with the iQcenter before registering for the exam.

You will be expected to pay for the exam on the day of the exam, regardless of whether or not you pass. The suggested retail price is $75, but each iQcenter determines its own fee for the exam; you could be expected to pay more for proctoring and administering costs, or less if the exam fee is incorporated into a classroom fee.

TAKE THE EXAM

The day of the exam you will want to be prepared by ensuring you have slept well the previous night, have eaten, and that you are dressed comfortably. Arrive at the test site approximately a half an hour before the scheduled exam time to ensure you have plenty of time to complete the log-on information, pay for the exam, and acquaint yourself with your surroundings.

You will need to bring payment for the exam and a valid picture ID. You may not bring any study or reference materials into the exam. As the exam is administered on a computer, you may not bring writing implements, calculators, or other test-taking materials.

If you do not pass the exam the first time, you can sign up to retake it as many times as needed to pass, but you will be charged each time you take it. No refunds will be given if you do not pass, and you may also be charged for a missed exam appointment depending on the iQcenter's policies.

Exam Specifics

☐ The first step is to log onto the exam. You will be asked to complete the candidate information section, which includes the necessary information for completing and mailing your certificate. Then the exam administrator will assist you in starting the exam.

☐ The first screens you see after you log on are directions and test-taking tips. You should read all of these, as it is important to become familiar with the exam environment. The timed portion of the exam does not include these start-up directional screens, so take your time and make sure you understand the directions before starting the exam.

☐ The overall exam is timed, although there is no time limit for each question. Most exams take an hour or less, but the allotted time depends on the subject and level. If you do not complete all of the exam questions within the given timeframe, you will lose points for any unanswered questions.

☐ There is an exam clock on the screen that can be turned on or off. The exam clock starts and stops while each question is loading, so the speed with which each question is loaded is not a factor in the time you have to complete the questions (i.e., people using slower computers are not penalized). The total time spent taking the exam will vary based on the speed of your computer, but the actual time you have to complete the exam will be consistent with anyone else taking the exam.

☐ Because you have to complete the exam in a certain amount of time, you will want to take into consideration the amount of time you have per question. You will not be graded on your efficiency (i.e., the time you take per question), but you will need to keep in mind that if you spend a lot of time on one question, that leaves you with less time for other questions. If you are truly stuck, you may want to skip a question.

☐ The exam is "live in the application," which means that you will work with an actual document, spreadsheet, presentation, etc. and must perform tasks on that document.

☐ Each question is comprised of several tasks listed in a pane at the bottom of the screen. You should complete the tasks in the order listed and make sure that you complete all of the tasks. You may need to scroll the pane to read all of the tasks in a question. It is a good idea to reread the entire question before advancing to the next question to ensure that you have completed all tasks. You will receive only partial credit for any question you do not complete in its entirety.

☐ The end result of your actions is what is scored when you advance to the next question. You will not lose points for any extra mouse clicks or movements as they relate to the task. You should undo any additional changes that are not part of the task that you might accidentally apply to the document. Because you will be marked down for any additional tasks that you perform, you can use the Reset button to return the document to its original state and redo the question from the beginning. Keep in mind that if you click the Reset button, all of your work on that question will be erased, and the clock does not restart.

☐ You cannot go back to a previous question. Be sure you have completed as much of the question as possible before advancing to the next question and that you have closed all dialog boxes, toolbars, Help windows, etc., that you might have opened unless instructed to keep them open.

☐ If the task requires typing, you will lose points for spelling mistakes.

☐ You can use any valid method available in the program to complete a task. For example, if asked to center text in a Word document, you can click a button on the Formatting toolbar or press [Ctrl][E]. If you press the [Spacebar] repeatedly to move the text to the center of the document, however, you will lose credit, as this is not an accurate centering method.

☐ You can use Office Help or any available Wizards during the exam. This will not count against you, but the time spent using Help or a Wizard may mean that you do not have time for a question at the end.

☐ If something happens to the exam environment, e.g, the program freezes, or there is a power failure, contact the exam administrator. He or she will restart the exam where you were before the exam was interrupted. This will not count against you.

Receive Exam Results

☐ Upon completing the exam or when time expires, your score will be immediately shown and you will know whether or not you have passed.

☐ You will be given a printout of your score to take with you. If you pass you can expect the certificate to be mailed to you within 2-3 weeks.

☐ The exam results are confidential.

☐ If you do not pass, keep in mind that the exams are challenging. Do not become discouraged. Remember, you can retake the exam as many times as you want, although you will need to pay for each test you take.

MICROSOFT WORD 2002 EXAM
REFERENCE
Getting Started with Word 2002

The Word MOUS exams assume a basic level of proficiency in Word. This section is intended to help you reference these basic skills while you are preparing to take the Word Core or Expert exams.

- ☐ Starting and exiting Word
- ☐ Viewing the Word window
- ☐ Using toolbars
- ☐ Using task panes
- ☐ Opening and closing documents
- ☐ Navigating in the document window
- ☐ Using views
- ☐ Using smart tags
- ☐ Getting Help
- ☐ Start and exit Word

START AND EXIT WORD

Start Word

Button Method
- ☐ Click the **Start button** `Start` on the Windows taskbar
- ☐ Point to Programs or **All Programs**
- ☐ Click **Microsoft Word**
  OR
- ☐ Double-click the **Microsoft Word program icon** on the desktop

Exit Word

Menu Method
- ☐ Click **File** on the menu bar, then click **Exit**

Button Method
- ☐ Click the **Close button** ☒ on the program window title bar

VIEW THE WORD WINDOW

Figure WD-1 Word Window

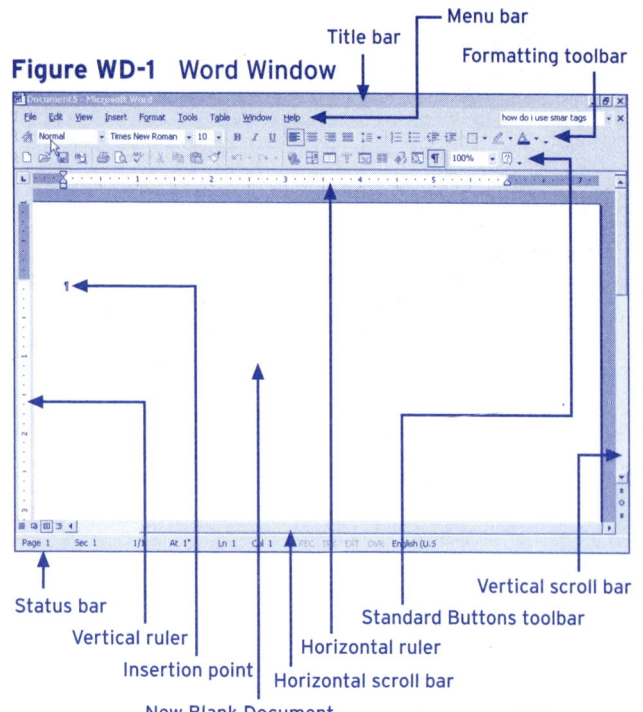

Menu bar

Title bar

Formatting toolbar

Vertical scroll bar

Standard Buttons toolbar

Horizontal ruler

Status bar

Vertical ruler

Insertion point   Horizontal scroll bar

New Blank Document

USE TOOLBARS

Display Toolbars

Menu Method

- ☐ Click **View** on the menu bar, point to **Toolbars**, then click the toolbar you want to display

  OR

- ☐ Right-click any toolbar, then click the toolbar you want to display on the shortcut menu

Customize Toolbars

Menu Method

- ☐ Click **Tools** on the menu bar, then click **Customize**, or click **View** on the menu bar, point to **Toolbars**, then click **Customize**, or right-click any toolbar, then click **Customize** on the shortcut menu
- ☐ In the Customize dialog box, select the appropriate options, then click **Close**

Button Method

- ☐ Click the **Toolbar Options button** 〉 of the toolbar to customize
- ☐ Point to **Add or Remove buttons**, then click **Customize**
- ☐ In the Customize dialog box, select the appropriate options, then click **Close**

Reposition Toolbars

Mouse Method

- ☐ Position the pointer in any blank area of the toolbar (not over a button)
- ☐ When the pointer changes to ✛, press and hold the mouse button
- ☐ Drag the toolbar to the desired location, then release the mouse button

USE TASK PANES

Menu Method

- ☐ If the task pane is not open, click **View** on the menu bar, then click **Task Pane** or right-click the toolbar, then click **Task Pane** on the shortcut menu
- ☐ Click the **Other Task Panes list arrow** ▼ on the task pane title bar, then click the appropriate task pane
- ☐ Click the **Back button** ◄ on the task pane title bar to return to the previously displayed task pane
- ☐ Click the **Close button** ✕ on the task pane title bar to close the task pane

OPEN AND CLOSE DOCUMENTS

Open a New Document

Menu Method
□ Click **File** on the menu bar, then click **New**
□ Click **Blank Document** under **New** in the New Document task pane

Button Method
□ Click the **New button** 🗋 on the Standard Buttons toolbar

Keyboard Method
□ Press **[Ctrl][N]**

Open an Existing Document

Menu Method
□ Click **File** on the menu bar, then click **Open**
□ In the Open dialog box, navigate to the appropriate drive and folder
□ Click the file, then click **Open**

Task Pane Method
□ Click a document under the Open a document section in the New Document task pane or click **More documents** under the Open a document section, then follow the second and third bullets in the Open an Existing Document Menu Method above

Button Method
□ Click the **Open button** 📂
□ Follow the second and third bullets in the Open an Existing Document Menu Method above

Keyboard Method
□ Press **[Ctrl][O]**
□ Follow the second and third bullets in the Open an Existing Document Menu Method above

Close Documents

Menu Method
□ Click **File** on the menu bar, then click **Close**
□ If prompted to save the file, click **Yes** or **No** as appropriate

Button Method
□ Click the **Close Window button** ✕ on the menu bar
□ If prompted to save the file, click **Yes** or **No** as appropriate

Keyboard Method
□ Press **[Ctrl][W]**
□ If prompted to save the file, click **Yes** or **No** as appropriate

NAVIGATE IN THE DOCUMENT WINDOW

Menu Method

☐ Click **Edit** on the menu bar, then click **Go To**

☐ On the Go to tab of the Find and Replace dialog box, select the appropriate options

Keyboard Method

☐ Use Table WD-1 as a reference

   OR

☐ Press **[Ctrl][G]**

☐ On the Go to tab of the Find and Replace dialog box, select the appropriate options

Scroll Bar Method

☐ Drag the scroll box in the scroll bar to move in the document without moving the insertion point

☐ Click above the scroll box in the vertical scroll bar to jump up a screen

☐ Click below the scroll box in the vertical scroll bar to jump down a screen

☐ Click the **up scroll arrow** in the vertical scroll bar to move up one line

☐ Click the **down scroll arrow** in the vertical scroll bar to move down one line

☐ Click the **Next Page button** ⬇ or the **Previous Page button** ⬆ on the vertical scroll bar to move to the next or previous page

Table WD-1: Navigation Keyboard Shortcuts

Key	Moves the insertion point
[Ctrl][Home]	To the beginning of the document
[Ctrl][End]	To the end of the document
[Home]	To the beginning of the current line
[End]	To the end of the current line
[Page Down], [Page Up]	Down or up one screen at a time
[→], [←]	To the right or left one character at a time
[Ctrl],[→] [Ctrl],[←]	To the right or left one word at a time
[↓],[↑]	Down or up one line

USE VIEWS

Table WD-2: Document Views

View	What you see	Button method (buttons located to the left of the horizontal scroll bar)	Menu method
Normal	Formatted text, but not headers, footers, or some graphics, does not show document as it would appear when printed	Normal View button	Click View on the menu bar, then click Normal
Web Layout view	Document as it would appear when published to a Web page	Web Layout View button	Click View on the menu bar, then click Web Layout
Print Layout view	Document as it would appear when printed	Print Layout View button	Click View on the menu bar, then click Print Layout
Outline view	Document headings indented to display the structure of the document	Outline View button	Click View on the menu bar, then click Outline
Zoom	Document magnified or shrunken to see more or less	Zoom list arrow 100% (on the Standard Buttons toolbar)	Click View on the menu bar, click Zoom, in the Zoom dialog box make the selection, then click OK

USE SMART TAGS

Button Method

☐ Move the pointer over text underlined with a purple dotted line until the **Smart Tag Actions button** appears

☐ Click to see the actions you can perform, then select an action

GET HELP

Menu Method

☐ Click **Help** on the menu bar, then click **Microsoft Word Help**

☐ Use Table WD-3 as a reference to select the most appropriate way to search for help using the Microsoft Word Help window

Button Method

☐ Click the **Microsoft Word Help button** 🔲 on the Standard Buttons toolbar

☐ Use Table WD-3 as a reference to select the most appropriate way to search for help using the Microsoft Word Help window
OR

☐ Click the **Ask a Question box** [Type a question for help ▾] on the menu bar

☐ Type your question, then press **[Enter]**

☐ Select the option you want from the drop down list, then read about your question in the Microsoft Word Help window, using Table WD-3 as a reference

Keyboard Method

☐ Press **[F1]**

☐ Use Table WD-3 as a reference to select the most appropriate way to search for help using the Microsoft Word Help window

Table WD-3: Microsoft Help Window Tabs

Tab	To use
Contents	Click the Expand indicator ⊞ next to each topic you want to explore further, then click the selection you want and read the results in the right pane
Answer Wizard	Type your question in the What would you like to do? text box, click **Search**, then read the results in the right pane
Index	Type the keyword(s) you want to search for in the Type keywords text box, click Search, then read the results in the right pane

Word CORE Exam Reference

Skill Sets:
1 Inserting and modifying text
2 Creating and modifying paragraphs
3 Formatting documents
4 Managing documents
5 Working with graphics
6 Workgroup collaboration

Word Skill Set 1: Inserting and Modifying Text

Insert, Modify, and Move Text and Symbols

Insert Text

Keyboard Method
- ☐ Click where you want to insert
- ☐ Type the words to insert, making sure to press **[Spacebar]** where appropriate to insert spaces between words and **[Enter]** to separate paragraphs

Insert Symbols

Menu Method
- ☐ Click where you want to insert the symbol
- ☐ Click **Insert** on the menu bar, then click **Symbol**
- ☐ In the Insert Symbol dialog box, select the appropriate symbol, click **Insert**, then click **Close**

Edit Text

Keyboard Method
Select text to be edited, or place the insertion point where you want to edit, then use the methods in Table WD-4 below to edit text.

Table WD-4: Editing Text

Method	Effect
Press [Backspace]	Deletes the character immediately to the left of the insertion point
Press [Delete]	Deletes the character immediately to the right of the insertion point
Select the text to delete, then start to type replacement text	The characters you type will replace all of the selected text

Cut and Paste Text

Menu Method

☐ Select the text to cut

☐ Click **Edit** on the menu bar, then click **Cut**, or right-click, then click **Cut** on the shortcut menu

☐ Click where you want to paste the text

☐ Click **Edit** on the menu bar, then click **Paste**

Button Method

☐ Select the text to cut

☐ Click the **Cut button** 🔲 on the Standard Buttons toolbar

☐ Click where you want to paste the text

☐ Click the **Paste button** 🔲 on the Standard Buttons toolbar

Keyboard Method

☐ Select the text to cut

☐ Press **[Ctrl][X]**

☐ Click where you want to paste the text

☐ Press **[Ctrl][V]**

Copy and Paste Text

Menu Method

☐ Select the text to copy

☐ Click **Edit** on the menu bar, click **Copy**, or right-click, then click **Copy** on the shortcut menu

☐ Click where you want to paste the text

☐ Click **Edit** on the menu bar, then click **Paste**

Button Method

☐ Select the text to copy

☐ Click the **Copy button** 🔲 on the Standard Buttons toolbar

☐ Click where you want to paste the text

☐ Click the **Paste button** 🔲 on the Standard Buttons toolbar

Keyboard Method

☐ Select the text to copy

☐ Press **[Ctrl][C]**

☐ Click where you want to paste the text

☐ Press **[Ctrl][V]**

Use the Paste Special Command

Menu Method

☐ Select the text to copy

☐ Click **Edit** on the menu bar, then click **Copy**

☐ Click where you want to paste the text

☐ Click **Edit** on the menu bar, then click **Paste Special**

☐ In the Paste Special dialog box, select the appropriate pasting option, then click **OK**

Find and Replace Text

Menu Method

- [ ] Click **Edit** on the menu bar, then click **Replace** to open the Find and Replace dialog box
- [ ] Type the appropriate text in the Find what text box
- [ ] Type the appropriate text in the Replace with text box, then click **Replace All** or **Find Next** to replace for each instance
- [ ] Click **Yes** if prompted to search document from the beginning
- [ ] Click **OK**, then click **Close** in the Find and Replace dialog box

Keyboard Method

- [ ] Press **[Ctrl][F]**
- [ ] In the Find and Replace dialog box, click the **Replace tab**
- [ ] Follow the steps in the second through fifth bullets in the Find and Replace Text Menu Method above
  OR
- [ ] Press **[Ctrl][H]** to open the Replace tab in the Find and Replace dialog box
- [ ] Follow the steps in the second through fifth bullets in the Find and Replace Text Menu Method above

Create AutoText Entries and Use AutoComplete

Menu Method

- [ ] Select the text you want to create an AutoText entry for
- [ ] Click **Insert** on the menu bar, point to **AutoText**, then click **New**
- [ ] In the Create AutoText dialog box, click **OK**
- [ ] Click where you want to insert the AutoText entry, type the first few letters
- [ ] When the AutoComplete ScreenTip appears, press **[Enter]** or **[Tab]** to complete the AutoText entry

Keyboard Method

- [ ] Select the text you want to create an AutoText entry for, then press **[Alt][F3]**
- [ ] Follow the steps in the third through fifth bullets in the Create AutoText Entries and Use AutoComplete Menu Method above

Use AutoCorrect

Menu Method

- [ ] Click **Tools** on the menu bar, then click **AutoCorrect Options**
- [ ] In the AutoCorrect dialog box, enter the text you want AutoCorrect to replace in the Replace text box
- [ ] Type the text to replace it with in the With text box, then click **Add**
- [ ] Click the appropriate check boxes to correct formatting and typing mistakes, then click **OK**

APPLY AND MODIFY TEXT FORMATS

Apply and Modify Character Formats

Select the text to which you want to apply a character format, then use Table WD-5 as a reference.

Table WD-5: Applying and Modifying Character Formats

Format	Button	Menu	Keyboard
Bold	Click the Bold button **B** on the Formatting toolbar	Click Format on the menu bar, click Font, click Bold under Font style, then click OK	Press [Ctrl][B]
Underline	Click the Underline button **U** on the Formatting toolbar	Click Format on the menu bar, click Font, click Underline under Font style, then click OK	Press [Ctrl][U]
Italic	Click the Italic button *I* on the Formatting toolbar	Click Format on the menu bar, click Font, click Italic under Font style, then click OK	Press [Ctrl][I]
Increase or decrease font size	Click the Font size button 10 ▾ on the Formatting toolbar, then click the desired font size	Click Format on the menu bar, click Font, click the desired font size under the Size section, then click OK	To increase: Press [Ctrl][right bracket] To decrease: Press [Ctrl][left bracket]

Use the Format Painter

Button Method
☐ Select the text with formatting you want to copy
☐ Click the **Format Painter button** 🖋
☐ Select the text to format
☐ To copy formatting for use in several locations, double-click 🖋, click each instance, then click 🖋 to turn the option off

Keyboard Method
☐ Select the text with formatting you want to copy
☐ Press **[Ctrl][Shift][C]**
☐ Select the text to format
☐ Press **[Ctrl][Shift][V]** for each instance

CORRECT SPELLING AND GRAMMAR USAGE

Correct Spelling and Grammar Errors

Menu Method

☐ Click **Tools** on the menu bar, then click **Spelling and Grammar**

☐ In the Spelling and Grammar dialog box, choose to ignore or change misspelled words, add words to the dictionary and accept or ignore grammar suggestion as appropriate

☐ When the spelling and grammar check is complete, click **OK** in the message box

Button Method

☐ Click the **Spelling and Grammar button** 🗹 on the Standard Buttons toolbar

☐ Follow the steps in the second and third bullets in the Correct Spelling and Grammar Errors Menu Method above

Keyboard Method

☐ Press **[F7]**

☐ Follow the steps in the second and third bullets in the Correct Spelling and Grammar Errors Menu Method above

Use the Thesaurus

Menu Method

☐ Select the word for which you want to find a synonym

☐ Click **Tools** on the menu bar, point to **Language**, then click **Thesaurus**

☐ In the Thesaurus dialog box, select the appropriate synonym, then click **Replace**
OR

☐ Right-click the word for which you want to find a synonym

☐ Point to **Synonyms** on the shortcut menu, then click the appropriate synonym, or click **Thesaurus**, then in the Thesaurus dialog box, select the appropriate synonym, then click **Replace**

Keyboard Method

☐ Select the word for which you want to find a synonym

☐ Press **[Shift][F7]**

☐ In the Thesaurus dialog box, select the appropriate synonym, then click **Replace**

APPLY FONT AND TEXT EFFECTS

Apply Character Effects

Menu Method

- ☐ Select the text to which you want to apply a character effect
- ☐ Click **Format** on the menu bar, then click **Font**, or right-click, then click **Font** on the shortcut menu
- ☐ In the Effects section of the Font dialog box, click the check boxes to apply appropriate formatting, then click **OK**

Keyboard Method

- ☐ Select the text to which you want to apply a character effect
- ☐ Press the keyboard combination to apply the appropriate character effect, using Table WD-6 as a reference

Table WD-6: Keyboard Methods for Applying Character Effects

Effect	Keyboard method
All Caps	[Ctrl][Shift][A]
Small Caps	[Ctrl][Shift][K]
Subscript	[Ctrl][=]
Superscript	[Ctrl][Shift][=]

Apply Text Animation

Menu Method

- ☐ Click **Format** on the menu bar, then click **Font**, or right-click, then click **Font** on the shortcut menu
- ☐ In the Fonts dialog box, click the **Text Effects tab**
- ☐ Click the appropriate animation, then click **OK**

Apply Highlighting

Button Method

- ☐ Select the text to highlight
- ☐ Click the **Highlight list arrow** on the Formatting toolbar, then click the appropriate color
  OR
- ☐ Click the **Highlight list arrow** on the Formatting toolbar, then click the appropriate color
- ☐ Click and drag over the text to highlight, then click when highlighting is complete

ENTER AND FORMAT DATE AND TIME

Insert a Date Field

Menu Method
☐ Click **Insert** on the menu bar, then click **Date and Time**
☐ In the Date and Time dialog box, click the appropriate date format, click the **Update automatically check box** to select it if necessary, then click **OK**

Keyboard Method
☐ Press **[Alt][Shift][D]**

Modify a Date Field

Menu Method
☐ Click the date to select it
☐ Right-click, then click **Edit Field** on the shortcut menu
☐ In the Field dialog box, select the appropriate formatting under Date formats, then click **OK**

APPLY CHARACTER STYLES

Apply Character Styles

Menu Method
☐ Select the text to format
☐ Click **Format** on the menu bar, then click **Styles and Formatting**
☐ In the Styles and Formatting task pane, select a style from the Pick a formatting to apply list, or click **New Style** to create a new style

Button Method
☐ Select the text to format
☐ Click the **Styles and Formatting button** 🖉 on the Formatting toolbar
☐ In the Styles and Formatting task pane, select a style from the Pick a formatting to apply list, or click **New Style** to create a new style

WORD SKILL SET 2: CREATING AND MODIFYING PARAGRAPHS

MODIFY PARAGRAPH FORMATS

Apply Paragraph Formats

Menu Method

- ☐ Select the text to format
- ☐ Click **Format** on the menu bar, then click **Paragraph**, or right-click, then click **Paragraph** on the shortcut menu
- ☐ In the Paragraph dialog box, click the appropriate options, then click **OK**

Button Method

- ☐ Position the insertion point in the paragraph to format
- ☐ Click the **Line Spacing list arrow** 📄 ▾ on the Formatting toolbar, then click the appropriate line spacing option

Modify Paragraph Alignment

Menu Method

- ☐ Select the text to format
- ☐ Click **Format** on the menu bar, then click **Paragraph**, or right-click, then click **Paragraph** on the shortcut menu
- ☐ In the Paragraph dialog box, click the **Indents and Spacing tab**
- ☐ Click the **Alignment list arrow**, then select the desired alignment using Table WD-7 as a reference

Button Method

- ☐ Select the text to format
- ☐ Click the appropriate button on the Formatting toolbar, using Table WD-7 as a reference

Keyboard Method

- ☐ Select the text to format
- ☐ Press the appropriate keyboard combination, using Table WD-7 as a reference

Table WD-7: Button and Keyboard Methods for Paragraph Alignment

Alignment	Button	Keyboard
Left-aligned	Click the **Align Left button** 📄 on the Formatting toolbar	[Ctrl][L]
Right-aligned	Click the **Align Right button** 📄 on the Formatting toolbar	[Ctrl][R]
Centered	Click the **Center button** 📄 on the Formatting toolbar	[Ctrl][E]
Justified	Click the **Justify button** 📄 on the Formatting toolbar	[Ctrl][J]

Apply Borders to Paragraphs

Menu Method
- ☐ Select the text you want to apply a border to
- ☐ Click **Format** on the menu bar, then click **Borders and Shading**
- ☐ In the Borders and Shading dialog box, click the **Borders tab** if necessary
- ☐ Select the appropriate option(s), then click **OK**

Button Method
- ☐ Select the text you want to apply a border to
- ☐ Click the **Borders list arrow** ☐▾ on the Formatting toolbar
- ☐ Click the appropriate option from the border options palette

Apply Shading to Paragraphs

Menu Method
- ☐ Select the text to shade
- ☐ Click **Format** on the menu bar, then click **Borders and Shading**
- ☐ In the Borders and Shading dialog box, click the **Shading tab** if necessary
- ☐ Select the appropriate option(s), then click **OK**

Set First-Line Indents

Menu Method
- ☐ Select the text to indent
- ☐ Click **Format** on the menu bar, then click **Paragraph**, or right-click, then click **Paragraph** on the shortcut menu
- ☐ In the Indentation section of the Paragraph dialog box, click the **Special list arrow**
- ☐ Click **First line**, then enter the appropriate indentation in the By text box
- ☐ Click **OK**

Button Method
- ☐ Select the paragraphs to indent
- ☐ Click the **Tab button** to the left of the ruler until you see the **First Line Indent marker** ▽
- ☐ Click the gray bottom border of the ruler where you want the First Line Indent marker to appear

Mouse Method
- ☐ Position ⬚ over the First Line Indent marker on the ruler until the Screen tip appears
- ☐ Press and hold the left mouse button
- ☐ Drag the First Line Indent marker to the appropriate location on the ruler

Indent Entire Paragraphs

Menu Method

☐ Select the paragraph to indent

☐ Click **Format** on the menu bar, then click **Paragraph**, or right-click, then click **Paragraph** on the shortcut menu

☐ In the Paragraph dialog box, click the **Indents and Spacing tab**

☐ Select the appropriate Left and Right indentations, then click **OK**

Button Method

☐ Select the paragraph to indent

☐ Click the **Increase Indent button** or the **Decrease Indent button** on the Formatting toolbar to change the indentation level from the left margin

☐ To indent from the right margin, position the pointer over the **Right Indent marker** △ on the right side of the ruler, then drag △ to the desired mark on the ruler

Set Hanging Indents

Menu Method

☐ Select the paragraph to indent

☐ Click **Format** on the menu bar, then click **Paragraph**, or right-click, then click **Paragraph** on the shortcut menu

☐ In the Paragraph dialog box, click the **Indents and Spacing tab** if necessary

☐ In the Indentation section, click the **Special list arrow**

☐ Click **Hanging**, enter the appropriate indentation in the By text box, then click **OK**

Button Method

☐ Select the paragraph to indent

☐ Point to the **Hanging Indent marker** △ on the left side of the ruler until the ScreenTip appears, then drag △ to the desired mark on the ruler

Keyboard Method

☐ Select the paragraph to indent

☐ Press **[Ctrl][T]** as many times as necessary

SET AND MODIFY TABS

Set Center Tabs

Menu Method

☐ Click **Format** on the menu bar, then click **Tabs**

☐ In the Tabs dialog box, type where you want the tab to be placed in the Tab stop position text box

☐ Click the **Center option button**, click **Set**, then click **OK**

Button Method

- ☐ Click the **Tab button** to the left of the horizontal ruler until ⬛ appears, then click the horizontal ruler where you want to place the tab

Modify Tabs

Menu Method

- ☐ Click **Format** on the menu bar, then click **Tabs**
- ☐ In the Tabs dialog box, type where you want the tab to be placed in the Tab stop position text box, click **Set**, then click **OK**

Button Method

- ☐ Position ▷ over the tab on the horizontal ruler
- ☐ Use ▷ to drag the tab to the desired location, or drag it off the ruler to delete it

APPLY BULLET, OUTLINE, AND NUMBERING FORMAT TO PARAGRAPHS

Create a Bulleted List

Menu Method

- ☐ Select the text to which you want to apply bullets, or click where you want to start a new bulleted list
- ☐ Click **Format** on the menu bar, then click **Bullets and Numbering**, or right-click, then click **Bullets and Numbering** on the shortcut menu
- ☐ In the Bullets and Numbering dialog box, click the **Bulleted tab**, select the appropriate option(s), then click **OK**
- ☐ To add a bullet to a new list, type the text, then press **[Enter]**
- ☐ To add a bullet to an existing list, position the insertion point at the end of the last item in the bulleted list, press **[Enter]**, then type the text for the new bullet item

Button Method

- ☐ Select the text to which you want to apply bullets, or click where you want to start a new bulleted list
- ☐ Click the **Bullets button** ▤ on the Formatting toolbar
- ☐ Follow the steps in the fourth and fifth bullets in the Create a Bulleted List Menu Method above

Create a Numbered List

Menu Method

- ☐ Select the text to which you want to add numbers, or click where you want to start a new numbered list
- ☐ Click **Format** on the menu bar, then click **Bullets and Numbering**, or right-click, then click **Bullets and Numbering** on the shortcut menu
- ☐ In the Bullets and Numbering dialog box, click the **Numbered tab**, select the appropriate option, then click **OK**

☐ To add a bullet to a new list, type the text, then press **[Enter]**

☐ To add a bullet to an existing list, place the insertion point at the end of the last numbered item in the list, press **[Enter]**, then type the text for the new numbered item

Button Method

☐ Select the text to which you want to add numbers, or click where you want to start a new numbered list

☐ Click the **Numbering button** 📄 on the Formatting toolbar

☐ Follow the steps in the fourth and fifth bullets in the Create a Numbered List Menu Method above

Create a Numbered List in Outline Style

Menu Method

☐ Select the text you want to list in outline

☐ Click **Format** on the menu bar, then click **Bullets and Numbering**, or right-click, then click **Bullets and Numbering** on the shortcut menu

☐ In the Bullets and Numbering dialog box, click the **Outline Numbered tab**, click the appropriate style, then click **OK**

☐ Click the text to outline, then click the **Promote button** 📄 on the Outlining toolbar or press **[Tab]** to move the selected text up a level, or click the **Demote button** 📄 on the Outlining toolbar or press **[Shift][Tab]** to move the text down a level

APPLY PARAGRAPH STYLES

Menu Method

☐ Click the paragraph to apply a style to

☐ Click **Format** on the menu bar, then click **Styles and Formatting**

☐ In the Styles and Formatting task pane, click the appropriate style from the Pick formatting to apply list

Button Method

☐ Click the paragraph to apply a style to

☐ Click the **Style list arrow** [Normal ▾] on the Formatting toolbar, then click the appropriate style

OR

☐ Click the paragraph to apply a style to

☐ Click the **Styles and Formatting button** 📄 on the Formatting toolbar

☐ In the Styles and Formatting task pane, click the appropriate style from the Pick formatting to apply list

WORD SKILL SET 3: FORMATTING DOCUMENTS

CREATE AND MODIFY A HEADER AND FOOTER

Create and Modify Headers and Footers

Menu Method

- ☐ Click **View** on the menu bar, then click **Header and Footer**
- ☐ In the Header and Footer dialog box, modify or enter the text to appear at the top of each page in the Header text box
- ☐ Click the **Switch Between Header and Footer button** 🔲 on the Header and Footer toolbar
- ☐ Modify or enter the text to appear at the bottom of each page in the Footer text box
- ☐ Click **Close** on the Header and Footer toolbar

APPLY AND MODIFY COLUMN SETTINGS

Create Columns for Existing Text

Menu Method

- ☐ Select the text to format as columns
- ☐ Click **Format** on the menu bar, then click **Columns**
- ☐ In the Columns dialog box, select the desired options, then click **OK**

Button Method

- ☐ Select the text to format as columns
- ☐ Click the **Columns button** 🔲 on the Formatting toolbar, then drag to select the desired number of columns

Modify Text Alignment in Columns

Menu Method

- ☐ Position the insertion point in the column to modify
- ☐ Click **Format** on the menu bar, then click **Columns**
- ☐ In the Columns dialog box, specify the appropriate alignment, then click **OK**

Create Columns Before Entering Text

Menu Method

- ☐ Click **Format** on the menu bar, then click **Columns**
- ☐ In the Columns dialog box, select the desired options, then click **OK**
- ☐ Start typing the text
- ☐ To insert a column break, click **Insert** on the menu bar, then click **Break**
- ☐ Click the **Column break option button** in the Break dialog box, then click **OK**

Button Method

☐ Click the **Columns button** 🖳 on the Formatting toolbar, then drag to select the desired number of columns

☐ Follow the steps in the third through fifth bullets in the Create Columns Before Entering Text Menu Method above

Revise Column Layout

Menu Method

☐ Select the column of text to be modified

☐ Click **Format** on the menu bar, then click **Columns**

☐ In the Columns dialog box, select the desired options, then click **OK**

Button Method

☐ Select the column of text to be modified

☐ Click the **Move Column marker** 🖳 on the ruler, then drag to the desired location

---

MODIFY DOCUMENT LAYOUT AND PAGE SETUP OPTIONS

Insert Page Breaks

Menu Method

☐ Click to the right of where the page break is to appear

☐ Click **Insert** on the menu bar, then click **Break**

☐ In the Break dialog box, click the **Page break option button** if necessary, then click **OK**

Keyboard Method

☐ Click to the right of where the page break is to appear, then press **[Ctrl][Enter]**

Insert Page Numbers

Menu Method

☐ Click **Insert** on the menu bar, then click **Page Numbers**

☐ In the Page Numbers dialog box, select the desired position, alignment, and format

☐ Click **OK**

Modify Page Margins

Menu Method

☐ Click **File** on the menu bar, then click **Page Setup**

☐ In the Page Setup dialog box, click the **Margins tab** if necessary

☐ Change the margins to the desired dimensions, then click **OK**

Button Method

☐ Click the margin marker you want to move on the ruler

☐ Using ◀▬▶, drag it to the desired location

Modify Page Orientation

Menu Method

- [ ] Click **File** on the menu bar, then click **Page Setup**
- [ ] In the Page Setup dialog box, click the **Margins tab** if necessary
- [ ] Click either the **Landscape** or **Portrait icon**, then click **OK**

CREATE AND MODIFY TABLES

Create Tables

Menu Method

- [ ] Click **Table** on the menu bar, point to **Insert**, then click **Table**
- [ ] In the Insert Table dialog box, select the desired number of columns and rows, then click **OK**
- [ ] To enter text in a table, press **[Tab]** or the arrow keys to navigate between cells

  OR

- [ ] Click **Table** on the menu bar, then click **Draw Table**
- [ ] Use $\mathscr{J}$ to draw rows and columns

Button Method

- [ ] Click the **Insert Table button** 🔲 on the Standard Buttons toolbar
- [ ] Drag to select the number of rows and columns on the Table palette

Modify Tables

Menu Method

- [ ] Click the table to be modified, click **Table** on the menu bar, then click **Table Properties**
- [ ] In the Table Properties dialog box, select the desired formatting options, using Table WD-8 as a reference

Table WD-8: Table Properties Dialog Box

Tab	Formatting options
Table	Set size of table, alignment of table on page, text wrapping options, and borders and shading
Row	Set row height, and specify how it breaks over pages
Column	Set column width
Cell	Set cell width and specify vertical alignment of cell contents

Button Method

Click the appropriate button on the Tables and Borders toolbar to modify the table, using Table WD-9 as a reference.

Table WD-9: Tables and Borders Toolbar Buttons for
Modifying Tables

Button	Effect
Merge Cells button 🔲	Merge cells
Split Cells button 🔲	Split cells
Change Text Direction button 🔲	Rotate the text
Distribute Columns Evenly button 🔲	Make columns the same size
Distribute Rows Evenly button 🔲	Make rows the same size

Mouse Method

☐ Move the pointer anywhere over the table to display the move and resize handles

☐ Position the pointer over the appropriate resize handle so that the pointer changes to ↖, ↓, ↗, or ↕, then drag in the appropriate direction to resize the table

Apply AutoFormats to Tables

Menu Method

☐ Select the table

☐ Click **Table** on the menu bar, then click **Table AutoFormat**

☐ In the Table AutoFormat dialog box, click the desired option(s) under Table styles, then click **Apply**

Button Method

☐ Select the table

☐ Click the **Table AutoFormat button** 🔲 on the Tables and Borders toolbar

☐ In the Table AutoFormat dialog box, click the desired option(s) under Table styles, then click **Apply**

Modify Table Borders and Shading

Menu Method

☐ Select the table

☐ Click **Format** on the menu bar, then click **Borders and Shading**, or right-click the **table**, then click **Borders and Shading** on the shortcut menu

☐ In the Borders and Shading dialog box, select the desired border options on the Borders tab

☐ Select the appropriate shading options on the Shading tab, then click **OK**

Button Method

- ☐ Select the table
- ☐ Click the **Border list arrow** ▣▾ on the Formatting toolbar, then click the desired border option from the palette
- ☐ Select the cells you wish to shade
- ☐ Click the **Fill Color list arrow** 🖫▾ on the Drawing toolbar, then select the desired color

Insert Rows and Columns in a Table

Menu Method

- ☐ Select the column or the row next to where you want the new column to appear
- ☐ Click **Table** on the menu bar, then point to **Insert**
- ☐ Click the appropriate option
  OR
- ☐ Select the column to the right of or the row below where you want the new column to appear
- ☐ Right-click, then click **Insert Columns** or **Insert Rows** on the shortcut menu

Button Method

- ☐ To add a column at the end of a table, use ↓ to click the Table Selector buttons
- ☐ Right-click, then click **Insert Columns** on the shortcut menu

Keyboard Method

- ☐ To insert a new row at the bottom of the table, click the far-right cell in the last row
- ☐ Press **[Tab]**

Delete Rows and Columns in a Table

Menu Method

- ☐ Select the row(s) or column(s) to delete
- ☐ Click **Table** on the menu bar, then point to **Delete**
- ☐ Click the appropriate option
  OR
- ☐ Select the column or row to delete
- ☐ Right-click, then click **Delete Columns** or **Delete Rows** on the shortcut menu

Keyboard Method

- ☐ Select the row(s) or column(s) to delete
- ☐ Press **[Ctrl][X]**

Modify Cell Formats in a Table

Menu Method

- ☐ Select the cell(s) to modify
- ☐ Click **Table** on the menu bar, then click **Table Properties**

☐ In the Table Properties dialog box, click the **Cell tab**

☐ Click the appropriate width or alignment option(s), then click **OK**

Button Method

☐ Select the Cell(s) to modify

☐ Click the Cell **Alignment list arrow** on the Tables and Borders toolbar

☐ Click the appropriate option

PREVIEW AND PRINT DOCUMENTS, ENVELOPES, AND LABELS

Preview a Document

Menu Method

☐ Click **File** on the menu bar, then click **Print Preview**

Button Method

☐ Click the **Print Preview button** 🖻 on the Standard Buttons toolbar

Keyboard Method

☐ Press **[Ctrl][F2]**

Print a Document

Menu Method

☐ Click **File** on the menu bar, then click **Print**

☐ In the Print dialog box, select the desired print settings, then click **OK**

Button Method

☐ Click the **Print button** 🖨 on the Standard Buttons toolbar

Keyboard Method

☐ Press **[Ctrl][P]**

☐ In the Print dialog box, select the desired print settings, then click **OK**

Print Envelopes and Labels

Menu Method

☐ Click **Tools** on the menu bar, point to **Letters and Mailings**, then click **Envelopes and Labels**

☐ In the Envelopes and Labels dialog box, click the **Envelopes tab** or the **Labels tab** to select your options and type your text

☐ Make sure you have the envelope or label paper in the manual feed tray of your printer, then click **Print**

WORD SKILL SET 4: MANAGING DOCUMENTS

MANAGE FILES AND FOLDERS FOR DOCUMENTS

Menu Method

- ☐ Click **File** on the menu bar, then click **Save As**
- ☐ In the Save As dialog box, click the **Create New Folder button** 🗀
- ☐ In the New Folder dialog box, type the folder name, then click **OK**
- ☐ In the Save As dialog box, type the document name in the File name text box
- ☐ Click **Save**

Keyboard Method

- ☐ Press **[F12]**
- ☐ Follow the steps in the second through fifth bullets of the Manage Files and Folders for Documents Menu Method above

CREATE DOCUMENTS USING TEMPLATES

Menu Method

- ☐ Click **File** on the menu bar, then click **New**
- ☐ In the New Document task pane, click **General Templates** under the New from template section
- ☐ In the Templates dialog box, select the appropriate tab and template, then click **OK**

SAVE DOCUMENTS USING DIFFERENT NAMES AND FILE FORMATS

Save a Document

Menu Method

- ☐ Click **File** on the menu bar, then click **Save**

Button Method

- ☐ Click the **Save button** 🖫 on the Standard Buttons toolbar

Keyboard Method

- ☐ Press **[Ctrl][S]**

Use Save As

Menu Method

- ☐ Click **File** on the menu bar, then click **Save As**
- ☐ In the Save As dialog box, click the **Save in list arrow** to select an appropriate drive and folder for your document
- ☐ Type the document name in the File name text box, then click **Save**

Keyboard Method

☐ Press **[F12]**

☐ Follow the steps in the second and third bullets of the Use Save As Menu Method above

Save a Document with a Different File Format

Menu Method

☐ Click **File** on the menu bar, then click **Save As**

☐ In the Save As dialog box, click the **Save as type list arrow**, then select the appropriate file format

☐ Click the **Save in list arrow** to select an appropriate drive and folder for your document

☐ Type the document name in the File name text box, then click **Save**

Keyboard Method

☐ Press **[F12]**

☐ Follow the steps in the second through fourth bullets of the Save a Document with a Different File Format Menu Method above

WORD SKILL SET 5: WORKING WITH GRAPHICS

INSERT IMAGES AND GRAPHICS

Insert Clips Using the Clip Organizer

Menu Method

- ☐ Position the insertion point in the document where the image is to appear
- ☐ Click **Insert** on the menu bar, point to **Picture**, then click **Clip Art**
- ☐ In the Insert Clip Art task pane, type the search criteria in the **Search** text text box, then click **Search**
- ☐ Position ☖ over the image you want, click the **list arrow**, then click **Insert**

Insert Images Not Stored in the Clip Organizer

Menu Method

- ☐ Position the insertion point in the document where the image is to appear
- ☐ Click **Insert** on the menu bar, point to **Picture**, then click **From File**
- ☐ In the Insert Picture dialog box, click the **Look in list arrow**, select the drive and location where the image is located, click the image, then click **Insert**

CREATE AND MODIFY DIAGRAMS AND CHARTS

Create an Organizational Chart

Menu Method

- ☐ Position the insertion point where the diagram is to appear in the document
- ☐ Click **Insert** on the menu bar, then click **Diagram**
- ☐ In the Diagram Gallery, click **Organizational Chart** if necessary, then click **OK**
- ☐ Click a chart text box, then type the text

Button Method

- ☐ Position the insertion point where the diagram is to appear in the document
- ☐ Click the **Insert Diagram or Organization Chart button** ☖ on the Drawing toolbar
- ☐ Follow the steps in the third and fourth bullets in the Create an Organizational Chart Menu Method above

Modify an Organizational Chart

Button Method

- ☐ Select the diagram
- ☐ Use ☖ to select and drag boxes to new locations or use the buttons from the Organization Chart toolbar to modify as appropriate using Table WD-10 as a reference

Table WD-10: Organizational Chart Modification Buttons

Button	Effect
Autoformat button 🔲	Accesses the Organization Chart Style Gallery to apply predefined formatting options
Select button Select ▾	Selects levels, branches, or lines in the chart
Insert Shape list arrow 🔲	Inserts Subordinate, Coworker, or Assistant chart text boxes
Layout list arrow Layout ▾	Changes the layout
Text Wrapping button 🔲	Changes the way text is wrapped

Create a Chart

Menu Method

- ☐ Click **Insert** on the menu bar, point to **Picture**, then click **Chart**
- ☐ Click **Chart** on the menu bar, then click **Chart Type**
- ☐ In the Chart Type dialog box, select the appropriate chart type, then click **OK**
- ☐ Type the information into the datasheet, then click the **Close button** on the datasheet

Modify a Chart

Menu Method

- ☐ Select the chart
- ☐ Click **Chart** on the menu bar, then click **Chart Options**, make the modifications in the Chart Options dialog box, then click **OK**

Button Method

- ☐ Select the chart
- ☐ Use the Chart toolbar buttons to modify the chart using Table WD-11 as a reference

Table WD-11: Chart Toolbar Buttons

Button	Effect
Chart Type list arrow 🔲 ▾	Select different types of charts
Legend button 🔲	Toggles the Legend on and off
Data Table 🔲	Displays a data table as part of the chart
By Row 🔲	Displays chart by datasheet rows
By Column 🔲	Displays chart by datasheet columns

Add and Format Objects in a Chart

Menu Method

- ☐ Right-click any label on the vertical axis, then click **Format Axis** on the shortcut menu
- ☐ In the Format Axis dialog box, make the appropriate modifications, then click **OK**
- ☐ Click **Chart** on the menu bar, then click **Chart Options**
- ☐ In the Chart Options dialog box, make the appropriate modifications, then click **OK**
- ☐ To add an object to a chart, click the appropriate button on the Drawing toolbar using Table WD-12 as a reference

Table WD-12: Inserting an Object into a Chart Using Drawing Toolbar Buttons

To insert a(n)	Click
Line	
Arrow	
Rectangle	
Oval	
Text box	

WORD SKILL SET 6: WORKGROUP COLLABORATION

COMPARE AND MERGE DOCUMENTS

Menu Method
- [ ] Click **Tools** on the menu bar, then click **Compare and Merge Documents**
- [ ] In the Compare and Merge Documents dialog box, select a document to compare
- [ ] Click the **Merge list arrow**, then click the appropriate merge option, using Table WD-13 as a reference
- [ ] Click the **Display for Review list arrow** `Final Showing Markup ▾` on the Reviewing toolbar, then click the appropriate option

Table WD-13: Methods for Merging Documents

Command	Results
Merge	Merges the changes into the original document, then opens the original document if it's not already open
Merge into current document	Merges the changes into the edited (current) document
Merge into new document	Merges the changes into a new document and leaves the original and edited documents unchanged; clicking the Legal blackline check box, then clicking Compare produces the same result

INSERT, VIEW, AND EDIT COMMENTS

Insert Comments

Menu Method
- [ ] Click next to or select the text the comment relates to
- [ ] Click **Insert** on the menu bar, click **Comment**
- [ ] Type the comment in the Comment text box

Button Method
- [ ] Click next to or select the text the comment refers to
- [ ] Click the **New Comment button** 🗊 on the Reviewing toolbar
- [ ] Type the comment in the Comment text box

View Comments

Menu Method
- [ ] Click **View** on the menu bar
- [ ] Click **Markup**

Button Method

☐ Click the **Show list arrow** `Show ▼` on the Reviewing toolbar, then click **Comments**

Edit Comments

Keyboard Method

☐ Click the **Comment text box**, then modify the comment text

CONVERT DOCUMENTS INTO WEB PAGES

Preview Documents as Web Pages

Menu Method

☐ Click **File** on the menu bar, then click **Web Page Preview**

Save Documents as Web Pages

Menu Method

☐ Click **File** on the menu bar, then click **Save as Web Page**
☐ In the Save As dialog box, type the filename in the File name text box
☐ Click **Save**

Word **EXPERT** Exam Reference

Skill Sets:

Word Skill Set 7: Customizing Paragraphs

Control Pagination

Control Page Breaks within Paragraphs

Menu Method

☐ Select the text to which you want the page breaks to apply, or deselect all text to apply the controls to the entire document
☐ Click **Format** on the menu bar, then click **Paragraph**, or right-click, then click **Paragraph** on the shortcut menu
☐ In the Paragraph dialog box, click the **Line and Page Breaks tab**
☐ Click the appropriate option, using Table WD-14 as a reference, then click **OK**

Table WD-14 Page Break Options in the Paragraph Dialog Box

Option	Effect
Widow/Orphan control	Prevents the last line of a paragraph from appearing at the top of a page (widow) or the first line of a paragraph from appearing at the bottom of a page (orphan)
Keep lines together	Prevents a page or column break from occurring within the selected paragraphs
Keep with next	If necessary, inserts a page break before the selected line(s), object, or paragraphs in order to keep them with the subsequent text
Page break before	Inserts a page break before each new paragraph

Control Page Breaks Between Paragraphs

Menu Method

☐ Select the text to which you want the page breaks to apply, or deselect all text to apply the controls to the entire document
☐ Click **Format** on the menu bar, then click **Paragraph**, or right-click, then click **Paragraph** on the shortcut menu
☐ In the Paragraph dialog box, click the **Line and Page Breaks tab**
☐ Click the **Keep with next check box**, then click **OK**

Control Line Breaks

Menu Method

- ☐ Select the text you want to hyphenate, or deselect all text to apply the hyphenation options to the entire document
- ☐ Click **Tools** on the menu bar, point to **Language**, then click **Hyphenation**
- ☐ In the Hyphenation dialog box, click the **Automatically hyphenate document check box**

OR

- ☐ Select the text you want to hyphenate, or deselect all text to apply the hyphenation options to the entire document
- ☐ Click **Tools** on the menu bar, point to **Language**, then click **Hyphenation**
- ☐ In the Hyphenation dialog box, click **Manual**
- ☐ If a Hyphenation message box appears, click **Yes** or **No** as appropriate for each instance, then click **OK** when the manual hyphenation is complete

OR

- ☐ Click **Format** on the menu bar, then click **Paragraph**, or right-click, then click **Paragraph** on the shortcut menu
- ☐ In the Paragraph dialog box, click the **Line and Page Breaks tab**
- ☐ Click the **Don't hyphenate check box**, then click **OK**

SORT PARAGRAPHS IN LISTS AND TABLES

Menu Method

- ☐ Select the list or table
- ☐ Click **Table** on the menu bar, then click **Sort**
- ☐ In the Sort Text or the Sort dialog box, select the order by which to sort and any other appropriate options, then click **OK**

Button Method

- ☐ Click the column in the table you want to sort
- ☐ Click the **Sort Ascending button** 🔼 or the **Sort Descending button** 🔽 on the Tables and Borders toolbar

WORD SKILL SET 8: FORMATTING DOCUMENTS

CREATE AND FORMAT DOCUMENT SECTIONS

Create Document Sections

Menu Method

- ☐ Click where you want to start a new section
- ☐ Click **Insert** on the menu bar, then click **Break**
- ☐ In the Break dialog box, click the appropriate Section break types option button, then click **OK**

Use Page Setup Options to Format Sections

Menu Method

- ☐ Position the insertion point in the section of the document you want to format
- ☐ Click **File** on the menu bar, then click **Page Setup**
- ☐ In the Page Setup dialog box, click the **Layout tab**
- ☐ Under Preview, click the **Apply to list arrow**, then click **This section**
- ☐ Select the appropriate options using Table WD-15 as a reference, then click **OK**

Table WD-15 Page Setup Dialog Box Layout tab Options

Dialog box section	Use to
Section	Define whether the section break is continuous, starts a new column, starts a new page, or will be on an odd or even page
Headers and footers	Define header and footer options such as whether the header and footers differ for odd and even pages, whether there is a different header and footer for the first page, and how far from the edge of the page the header and footer appear
Page	Select vertical alignment options: top, center, justified, or bottom
Preview	See a sample of the formatting options, as well as apply the options to the current section, the whole document, or from this point forward. Also can choose options for line numbers and page borders

Verify Paragraph and Character Formats

Menu Method

- ☐ Click **Format** on menu bar, then click **Reveal Formatting**
- ☐ In the Reveal Formatting task pane, click the **Font** and/or the **Paragraph Expand indicators** ⊞
- ☐ View the formatting options displayed in the task pane

Clear Formatting

Task Pane Method

☐ Select the formatted text
☐ Open the Reveal Formatting task pane if necessary
☐ Position the pointer over the **Selected text sample box**
☐ Click the **list arrow**, then click **Clear Formatting**

OR

☐ Select the formatted text
☐ Open the Styles and Formatting task pane if necessary
☐ Click **Clear Formatting** from the Pick a formatting to apply list box

Button Method

☐ Select the formatted text
☐ Click the **Style list arrow** `Normal ▾` on the Formatting toolbar, then click **Clear Formatting**

CREATE AND APPLY CHARACTER AND PARAGRAPH STYLES

Create Character and Paragraph Styles

Menu Method

☐ Click **Format** on the menu bar, then click **Styles and Formatting**
☐ In the Styles and Formatting task pane, click **New Style**
☐ In the New Style dialog box, type the name of the style in the Name text box, click the **Style type list arrow**, then click **Character** or **Paragraph**
☐ Select the appropriate formatting options using Table WD-16 as a reference, then click **OK**

Table WD-16 Formatting Options in the New Style Dialog Box

Button	Used to	Applies to
Font Type button `Times New Roman ▾`	Change the font type	Paragraph and Character
Font Size button `10 ▾`	Increase or decrease the font size	Paragraph and Character
Bold button **B**	Make text appear as **bold**	Paragraph and Character
Italic button *I*	Make text appear as *Italic*	Paragraph and Character
Underline button U	Make text appear as underlined	Paragraph and Character
Font Color button A ▾	Change the font color	Paragraph and Character
Align Left button	Align text with the left margin	Paragraph only
Center button	Align text in the center of the margins	Paragraph only
Align Right button	Align text with the right margin	Paragraph only
Justify button	Align text to the left and right margins	Paragraph only

Table WD-16 Formatting Options in the New Style Dialog Box (continued)

Button	Used to	Applies to
Single Space ▬ button	Space the lines without extra lines between them	Paragraph only
1.5 Space button ═	Adjust the spacing so that one and a half blank lines are inserted between each line of text	Paragraph only
Double Space ═ button	Adjust the spacing so that two blank lines are inserted between each line of text	Paragraph only
Increase Paragraph Spacing button	Increase space between paragraphs; click as many times as necessary until sample box matches desired spacing	Paragraph only
Decrease Paragraph Spacing button	Decrease space between paragraphs; click as many times as necessary until sample box matches desired spacing	Paragraph only
Decrease Indent button	Move the paragraph closer to the left margin; click as many times as necessary until sample box matches desired indentation	Paragraph only
Increase Indent button	Move the paragraph away from the left margin; click as many times as necessary until sample box matches desired indentation	Paragraph only

Button Method

□ Click the **Styles and Formatting button** 🖺 on the Formatting toolbar
□ Follow the second through fourth bullets in the Creating Character and Paragraph Styles Menu Method above

Apply Character and Paragraph Styles

Menu Method

□ Select the text to format
□ Click **Format** on the menu bar, then click **Styles and Formatting**
□ In the Styles and Formatting task pane, click the appropriate format in the Pick formatting to apply list box

Button Method

□ Select the text to format
□ Click the **Styles and Formatting button** 🖺 on the Formatting toolbar
□ In the Styles and Formatting task pane, click the appropriate format in the Pick formatting to apply list box

OR

□ Select the text to format
□ Click the **Style list arrow** Normal ▾ on the Formatting toolbar
□ Select the appropriate style

CREATE AND UPDATE DOCUMENT INDEXES AND TABLES OF CONTENTS, FIGURES, AND AUTHORITIES

Create an Index

Menu Method

☐ Select the text you want to reference as a main or subentry in the index
☐ Click **Insert** on the menu bar, point to **Reference**, then click **Index and Tables**
☐ In the Index and Tables dialog box, click the **Index tab** if necessary, then click **Mark Entry**
☐ In the Mark Index Entry dialog box, click the appropriate options, then click **Mark**
☐ Repeat for each word or phrase in the document that you want indexed, then click **Close** in the Mark Index Entry dialog box
☐ Position the insertion point where you want the index to appear
☐ Click **Insert** on the menu bar, point to **Reference**, then click **Index and Tables**
☐ In the Index and Tables dialog box, click the **Index tab** if necessary
☐ Select the appropriate options, then click **OK**

Keyboard Method

☐ Select the text you want to reference as a main or subentry in the index
☐ Press **[Alt][Shift][X]** to mark the text as an index entry
☐ Follow the steps in the fourth through ninth bullets in the Create an Index Menu Method above

Update an Index

Keyboard Method

☐ Make the changes using Table WD-17 as a reference

Table WD-17 Index Updating Options

If you want to make this change	Do this
Delete an entry	☐ Select the entry in the index, then press **[Delete]**
Change an entry	☐ Double-click the text in quotes (for example, {·XE·"View"·}) after the reference in the text to edit how the reference will appear in the index ☐ Right-click any **field** in the index, then click **Update Field** on the shortcut menu, or place the insertion point in the Index, then press **[F9]**
Add an entry	☐ See the Activity "Create an Index" to add an entry ☐ Right-click any field in the index, then click **Update Field** on the shortcut menu, or place the insertion point in the Index, then press **[F9]**

Table WD-17 Index Updating Options (continued)

If you want to make this change	Do this
Format an entry	☐ Select an index entry ☐ Click Insert on the menu bar, point to Reference, then click Index and Tables or right-click an entry, click Edit Field on the shortcut menu, then click Index in the Field dialog box ☐ In the Index and Tables or Index dialog box, click Modify ☐ In the Style dialog box, select the style to apply, or click Modify, then make the style modifications in the Modify Style dialog box, then click OK ☐ Click OK in the Style dialog box, then click OK in the Index and Tables or Index dialog box ☐ Click OK in the message box to replace the existing index if necessary

INSERT A TABLE OF CONTENTS

Menu Method

☐ Position the insertion point in the document where you want the table of contents to appear
☐ Click **Insert** on the menu bar, point to **Reference**, then click **Index and Tables**
☐ In the Index and Tables dialog box, click the **Table of Contents tab**
☐ Select the appropriate options, then click **OK**

Update a Table of Contents

Menu Method

☐ Make the appropriate modifications to the document
☐ Right-click any field in the table of contents, then click **Update Field** on the shortcut menu
☐ In the Update Table of Contents dialog box, click the appropriate option button, then click **OK**

Keyboard Method

☐ Make the appropriate modifications to the document
☐ Position the insertion point in the Table of Contents, then press **[F9]**
☐ In the Update Table of Contents dialog box, click the appropriate option button, then click **OK**

Insert a Table of Figures

Menu Method

☐ Position the insertion point below or above the figure
☐ Click **Insert** on the menu bar, point to **Reference**, then click **Caption**
☐ In the Caption dialog box, click the appropriate options, then click **OK**

☐ If appropriate, type a textual caption after the newly added figure number in the document
☐ Repeat the first through fourth bullets for each figure
☐ Click where you want the table of figures to appear
☐ Click **Insert** on the menu bar, point to **Reference**, then click **Index and Tables**
☐ In the Index and Tables dialog box, click the **Table of Figures tab**, click the appropriate options, then click **OK**

Update a Table of Figures

Menu Method

☐ Insert a new figure
☐ Position the insertion point below or above the figure
☐ Click **Insert** on the menu bar, point to **Reference**, then click **Caption**
☐ In the Caption dialog box, click the appropriate options, then click **OK**
☐ If appropriate, type a textual caption after the newly added figure number in the document
☐ Right-click a field in the Table of Figures, then click **Update Field** on the shortcut menu
☐ In the Update Table of Figures dialog box, click the appropriate option button, then click **OK**

Keyboard Method

☐ Follow the first through fifth bullets in the Update a Table of Figures Menu Method above
☐ Position the insertion point in the Table of Figures, then press **[F9]**
☐ In the Update Table of Figures dialog box, click the appropriate option button, then click **OK**

Create a Table of Authorities

Menu Method

☐ Select the text you want to cite
☐ Click **Insert** on the menu bar, point to **Reference**, then click **Index and Tables**
☐ In the Index and Tables dialog box, click the **Table of Authorities tab**, then click **Mark Citation**
☐ In the Mark Citation dialog box, click the appropriate options, click **Mark**, then click **Close** in the Mark Citation dialog box
☐ For each additional word or phrase in the document that you want indexed, select the text, then repeat the first through fourth bullets above
☐ Position the insertion point where you want the Table of Authorities to appear
☐ Click **Insert** on the menu bar, point to **Reference**, then click **Index and Tables**
☐ In the Index and Tables dialog box, click the **Table of Authorities tab** if necessary, select the appropriate options, then click **OK**

Keyboard Method

☐ Select the text you want to cite
☐ Press **[Alt][Shift][I]** to mark the text as a citation
☐ Follow the steps in the fourth through eighth bullets in the Create a Table of Authorities Menu Method above

Update a Table of Authorities

Menu Method

☐ Make the appropriate modifications to the document
☐ Right-click any **field** in the table of authorities, then click **Update Field** on the shortcut menu

Keyboard Method

☐ Make the appropriate modifications to the document
☐ Position the insertion point in the table of authorities, then press **[F9]**

CREATE CROSS-REFERENCES

Keyboard Method

☐ Click where you want the cross-reference to appear, then type the text for the reference
☐ Click **Insert** on the menu bar, point to **Reference**, then click **Cross-reference**
☐ In the Cross-reference dialog box, select the appropriate options, click **Insert**, then click **Close**

ADD AND REVISE ENDNOTES AND FOOTNOTES

Create Footnotes and Endnotes

Menu Method

☐ Click where you want the footnote to reference
☐ Click **Insert** on the menu bar, point to **Reference**, then click **Footnote**
☐ In the Footnote and Endnote dialog box, select the appropriate location and format options, then click **Insert**
☐ If you are in Normal view, type the text in the Footnote or Endnotes pane, then click the **Close button** in the Footnote or Endnote pane; if you are in Print Layout view, type the footnote or endnote text

Revise Footnotes and Endnotes

Menu Method

☐ In Print Layout view, click **Edit** on the menu bar, then click **Go To**
☐ In the Find and Replace dialog box, click **Footnote** or **Endnote** in the Go to what list
☐ In the Enter footnote number or Enter endnote number text box, type the number of the footnote or endnote you want to edit

☐ Click **Go To**, double-click the **footnote** or **endnote** you wish to format, select the text to edit, then make edits to the footnote or endnote text

OR

☐ In Normal view, click **View** on the menu bar, then click **Footnotes**
☐ If the Footnotes dialog box opens, click the appropriate option button
☐ Edit the text in the Footnote or Endnote pane, then click the **Close button** in the Footnote or Endnote pane

Keyboard Method

☐ In Print Layout view, double-click the footnote or endnote to revise
☐ Make the changes to the text

OR

☐ In Normal view, double-click the footnote or endnote number
☐ Make the changes to the text in the Footnote or Endnotes pane, then click the **Close button** in the Footnote or Endnote pane

CREATE AND MANAGE MASTER DOCUMENTS AND SUBDOCUMENTS

Create and Open Master Documents

Menu Method

☐ Click **View** on the menu bar, then click **Outline**
☐ Select the text, then click the appropriate button on the Outlining toolbar to promote or demote headings as necessary to create the master document, using Table WD-18 as a reference

Button Method

☐ Click the **Outline View button** 🔳 on the status bar
☐ Select the text, then click the appropriate button on the Outlining toolbar to promote or demote headings as necessary to create the master document, using Table WD-18 as a reference

Table WD-18 Outlining Toolbar Buttons

Button	Effect
Promote to Heading 1 button 🔄	Change the text to the highest header level
Promote button ◀	Change the text to the next highest header level
Outline Level list arrow Body text ▾	Use to select the level by name
Demote button ▶	Change the text to the next lowest header level
Demote to Body Text button ▶	Change the text to body text

Create Subdocuments

Menu Method

☐ Select the text you want to make into a subdocument, then click the **Create Subdocument button** 🔳 on the Outlining toolbar

☐ Click **File** on the menu bar, click **Save As**, navigate to the appropriate drive and folder, enter the appropriate filename in the File name text box, then click **Save**

Close and Open Subdocuments

Button Method

☐ Click the **Collapse Subdocuments button** 🔁 to close all subdocuments
☐ Click the **Expand Subdocuments button** 🔁 to open all subdocuments

Manage Master Documents and Subdocuments

Table WD-19 Managing Master Documents and Subdocuments

Task	Method
Merge subdocuments	Select both subdocuments in the Outline pane by pressing and holding [Shift], then click the Merge Subdocument button 🗋 on the Outlining toolbar
Split an outlining level into its own subdocument	Click the Expand indicator ⊞ next to the subdocument you want to split, then click the Split Subdocument button 🗋 on the Outlining toolbar
Move a subdocument	Drag the subdocument icon 🔢 until the vertical line indicator is below where you want it to appear (*Note*: moving it within a subdocument will create a subdocument within the subdocument)
Remove a subdocument from its master document and combine the text into the master document	Click the Subdocument icon 🔢 for the subdocument, then click the Remove Subdocument **button** 🔁 on the Outlining toolbar
Insert a new subdocument	Position the insertion point where you want the new subdocument to appear, click the Insert Subdocument button 🔢 in the Insert Subdocument dialog box, make sure that the appropriate drive and folder are listed in the Look in box, click the **filename**, then click Open

MOVE WITHIN DOCUMENTS

Create Bookmarks

Menu Method

☐ Select the text to bookmark
☐ Click **Insert** on the menu bar, then click **Bookmark**
☐ In the Bookmark dialog box, type the bookmark name (without using spaces and beginning with a letter), then click **Add**

Use Bookmarks

Menu Method

- ☐ Click **Edit** on the menu bar, then click **Go To**
- ☐ In the Find and Replace dialog box, click **Bookmark** in the Go to what list box
- ☐ Click the **Enter bookmark name list arrow**, then click the name of the bookmark
- ☐ Click **Go To**, then click **Close**

Keyboard Method

- ☐ Press **[Ctrl][G]**
- ☐ Follow the steps in the second through fourth bullets in the Use Bookmarks Menu Method above

Use the Document Map

Menu Method

- ☐ Click **View** on the menu bar, then click **Document Map**
- ☐ In the left pane of the Document Map, click the appropriate heading to jump to that location in the document
- ☐ Right-click the Document Map, then click the appropriate option from the shortcut menu to display, expand, or collapse headings

Button Method

- ☐ Click the **Document Map button** 🔲 on the Standard Buttons toolbar
- ☐ Click the **Expand indicator** ⊞ next to a header in the Document Map to display the subheadings
- ☐ Click the **Collapse Indicator** ⊟ next to a header in the Document Map to collapse the subheadings

CREATE AND MODIFY FORMS USING VARIOUS FORM CONTROLS

Create Forms

Button Method

- ☐ Position the insertion point in the document where you want to insert the form
- ☐ Click the appropriate field type button on the Forms toolbar, using the first three rows of Table WD-20 as a reference
- ☐ Click the **Form Field Options button** 🔲, or right-click the field, then click **Properties** on the shortcut menu
- ☐ In the Form Field Options dialog box, select the appropriate options, then click **OK**

Table WD-20 Form Toolbar Buttons

Button	Effect
Text Form Field button `abl`	Add a text field form control
Drop-Down Form Field button	Add a drop-down list field form control
Check Box Form Field button `☑`	Add a check box field form control
Form Field Shading button `a`	Turn shading off in the form fields
Insert Table button `▢`	Insert a table
Insert Frame button	Insert a frame

Modify Forms

Button Method

☐ Use Table WD-20 as a reference to modify the form

Protect Forms and Prepare for Distribution

Menu Method

☐ Click **Tools** on the menu bar, then click **Protect Document**
☐ In the Protect Document dialog box, select the appropriate options, and
   enter a password if necessary in the Password (optional) text box, then
   click **OK**
☐ If the Confirm Password dialog box appears, type the password in the In
   the Reenter password to open text box, then click **OK**

WORD SKILL SET 9: CUSTOMIZING TABLES

USE EXCEL DATA IN TABLES

Link Excel Data Using the Paste Command

Menu Method

- ☐ Start Excel and open the file that contains the data you want to use
- ☐ Select the cell or range you want to link, click **Edit** on the menu bar, then click **Copy**
- ☐ Activate the Word program window
- ☐ Position the insertion point in the Word document where you want the Excel table to appear, click **Edit** on the menu bar, then click **Paste**
- ☐ Click the **Paste Options button** 🔲 that appears in the document below the pasted data
- ☐ Click the **Keep Source Formatting and Link to Excel option button** or the **Match Destination Table Style and Link to Excel option button** as appropriate

Button Method

- ☐ Start Excel and open the file that contains the data you want to use
- ☐ Select the cell or range you want to link, then click the **Copy button** 🔲 on the Excel Standard Buttons toolbar
- ☐ Activate the Word program window
- ☐ Position the insertion point in the Word document where you want the Excel table to appear, then click the **Paste button** 🔲 on the Word Standard Buttons toolbar
- ☐ Follow the fifth and sixth bullets in the Link Excel Data Using the Paste Command Menu Method above

Keyboard Method

- ☐ Start Excel and open the file that contains the data you want to use
- ☐ Select the cell or range you want to link, then press **[Ctrl][C]**
- ☐ Activate the Word program window
- ☐ Position the insertion point in the Word document where you want the Excel table to appear, then press **[Ctrl][V]**
- ☐ Follow the fifth and sixth bullets in the Link Excel Data Using the Paste Command Menu Method above

Embed Excel Data in a Word Document

Menu Method

- ☐ Start Excel and open the file that contains the data you want to use
- ☐ Select the cell or range you want to embed, click **Edit** on the menu bar, then click **Copy**
- ☐ Activate the Word program window
- ☐ Position the insertion point in the Word document where you want the Excel table to appear, click **Edit** on the menu bar, then click **Paste**
- ☐ Click the **Paste Options button** 🔲 that appears in the document below the pasted data

☐ Click the **Keep Source Formatting option button**, the **Match Destination Table Style option button**, or the **Keep Text Only option button** as appropriate

Button Method

☐ Start Excel and open the file that contains the data you want to use
☐ Select the cell or range you want to embed, then click the **Copy button** 🖽 on the Excel Standard Buttons toolbar
☐ Activate the Word program window
☐ Position the insertion point in the Word document where you want the Excel table to appear, then click the **Paste button** 🖺 on the Word Standard Buttons toolbar
☐ Follow the fifth and sixth bullets in the Embed Excel Data in a Word Document Menu Method above

Keyboard Method

☐ Start Excel and open the file that contains the data you want to use
☐ Select the cell or range you want to embed, then press **[Ctrl][C]**
☐ Activate the Word program window
☐ Position the insertion point in the Word document where you want the Excel table to appear, then press **[Ctrl][V]**
☐ Follow the fifth and sixth bullets in the Embed Excel Data in a Word Document Menu Method above

PERFORM CALCULATIONS IN WORD TABLES

Use Formulas in Tables

Menu Method

☐ Click the table cell where you want the formula to appear, click **Table** on the menu bar, then click **Formula**
☐ In the Formula dialog box, click the **Formula box**, type **=** (equal sign), click the **Paste function list arrow**, click the appropriate function, then type the rest of the formula as appropriate
☐ Click **OK**

Button Method

☐ Click the table cell where you want the formula to appear
☐ Click the **AutoSum button** Σ on the Tables and Borders toolbar to quickly total a row or column

Merge Table Cells

Menu Method

☐ Select the cells to merge
☐ Click **Table** on the menu bar, then click **Merge Cells**

Button Method

☐ Select the cells to merge
☐ Click the **Merge Cells button** 🖽 on the Tables and Borders toolbar

Split Table Cells

Menu Method

☐ Select the cell(s) to split
☐ Click **Table** on the menu bar, then click **Split Cells**
☐ In the Split Cells dialog box, enter the number of rows and columns, then click **OK**

Button Method

☐ Select the cell(s) to split
☐ Click the **Split Cells button** 🖾 on the Tables and Formatting toolbar
☐ In the Split Cells dialog box, enter the number of rows and columns, then click **OK**

WORD SKILL SET 10: CREATING AND MODIFYING GRAPHICS

CREATE, MODIFY, AND POSITION GRAPHICS

Create Graphics in a Document

Button Method

☐ Click the appropriate button on the Drawing toolbar, using Table WD-12 as a reference
☐ Use $+$ to drag the shape to the correct size
☐ To create a perfect shape, click the appropriate button using Table WD-21 as a reference, then press and hold **[Shift]** while dragging on the Drawing Canvas

Table WD-21 Creating a Perfect Shape

Drawing toolbar button	Shape
╲ Line button	Straight line
▢ Rectangle button	Square
◯ Oval button	Circle

Insert Graphics in a Document

Menu Method

☐ Click **Insert** on the menu bar, point to **Picture**, then click the appropriate menu command using Table WD-22 as a reference

Button Method

☐ Click the appropriate button on the Drawing toolbar, then follow the steps using Table WD-22 as a reference

Table WD-22 Inserting a Graphic in a Document

Menu Command	Drawing Toolbar Button	Steps
Clip Art	Insert Clip Art button 🖼	☐ If prompted to add Clips to Organizer, click the Later button ☐ In the Insert Clip Art task pane, enter the search criteria in the Search text text box, then click Search ☐ Position the pointer over the image, click the list arrow, then click Insert
From File	Insert Picture 🖼	☐ In the Insert Picture dialog box, navigate to the appropriate drive and folder, click the image, then click Insert

Table WD-22 Inserting a Graphic in a Document (continued)

Menu Command	Drawing Toolbar Button	Steps
WordArt	Insert WordArt	☐ In the WordArt Gallery, click the WordArt shape, then click OK ☐ In the Edit WordArt Text dialog box, enter the text and select the appropriate formatting options, then click OK
Chart		☐ See the Activity "Create a Chart" in Word Skill Set 5
Organization Chart	Insert Diagram or Organization Chart button	☐ See the Activity "Create an Organization Chart" in Word Skill Set 5
New Drawing		☐ See the Activity "Create Graphics in a Document" in Word Skill Set 10

Modify Graphics in a Document

Menu Method

☐ Select the graphic, click **Format** on the menu bar, then click *Object* (where *object* is the element you are formatting), or right-click the graphic, then click **Format** *Object*

☐ In the Format *Object* dialog box, make the appropriate selections, then click **OK**

Button Method

☐ Select the graphic to modify, then use Table WD-23 as a reference

Table WD-23 Methods for Modifying Graphics

Effect	Method
Group multiple objects together	☐ Select each object, click the Draw button Draw ▼ on the Drawing toolbar, then click Group
Ungroup objects	☐ Select the grouped objects, click the Draw button Draw ▼ on the Drawing toolbar, then click Ungroup
Order	☐ Select the object, click the Draw button Draw ▼ on the Drawing toolbar, point to Order, then click the appropriate option
Grid	☐ Select the object, click the Draw button Draw ▼ on the Drawing toolbar, then click Grid ☐ In the Drawing Grid dialog box, click the appropriate options, then click OK
Nudge	☐ Select the object, click the Draw button Draw ▼ on the Drawing toolbar, point to Nudge, then click the appropriate option

Table WD-23 Methods for Modifying Graphics (continued)

Effect	Method
Align or Distribute	☐ Select the object, click the Draw button `Draw ▾` on the Drawing toolbar, point to Align or Distribute, then click the appropriate option
Rotate or Flip	☐ Click the object to rotate, position the pointer over the green Rotate handle so that it changes to 🔄, then drag the handle to rotate the object as desired OR ☐ Click the Draw button `Draw ▾` on the Drawing toolbar, point to Rotate or Flip, then click the appropriate option on the Rotate or Flip submenu
Text Wrap	☐ Select the object, click the Draw button `Draw ▾` on the Drawing toolbar, point to Text Wrapping, then click the appropriate option on the Text Wrapping submenu
Reroute Connectors	☐ Select one of the connected objects, click the Draw button `Draw ▾` on the Drawing toolbar, then click Reroute Connectors
Edit Points	☐ Select the object, click the Draw button `Draw ▾` on the Drawing toolbar, then click Edit Points

Add Text to Graphics in a Document

Button Method

☐ Click the **Text Box button** 📧 on the Drawing toolbar
☐ Drag ✛ to create the text box
☐ Type the text to appear in the text box

Position Graphics in a Document

Keyboard Method

☐ Select the graphic
☐ Using ✛, drag the graphic to position it

Button Method

☐ Click the **Draw button** `Draw ▾` on the Drawing toolbar, then click the appropriate option, using Table WD-23 as a reference

CREATE AND MODIFY CHARTS USING DATA FROM OTHER APPLICATIONS

Create Charts Using Data from Other Applications

Menu Method

☐ Click **Insert** on the menu bar, then click **Object**
☐ In the Object dialog box, click **Microsoft Graph Chart** in the Object type list box, then click **OK**, or click **Insert** on the menu bar, point to **Picture**, then click **Chart**
☐ Select all of the cells in the datasheet
☐ Click **Edit** on the menu bar, then click **Import File**

☐ In the Import File dialog box, navigate to the appropriate drive and folder, click the **file**, then click **Open**
☐ In the Import Data Options dialog box, click the worksheet in the workbook that contains the data to import, make sure the **Overwrite existing cells check box** is selected, then click **OK**

Modify a Chart

Menu Method

☐ Select the chart
☐ Click **Chart** on the menu bar, then click **Chart Options**
☐ In the Chart Options dialog box, select the appropriate options, then click **OK**

Resize a Chart

Mouse Method

☐ Select the chart
☐ Move the pointer over any sizing handle on the chart until it changes to ·the appropriate pointer, using Table WD-24 below as a reference
☐ Press and hold the left mouse button while you drag to resize the chart, then release the mouse button

Table WD-24 Resize Pointers

Pointer	Used to
↖ or ↗	Resize proportionally
↔	Resize horizontally
	Resize vertically

Change a Chart Type

Menu Method

☐ Select the chart
☐ Click **Chart** on the menu bar, then click **Chart Type**, or right-click, then click **Chart Type** on the shortcut menu
☐ In the Chart Type dialog box, make the appropriate selections, then click **OK**

Format Charts and Chart Text

Menu Method

☐ Click the appropriate chart object to select it (in the following steps, *object* refers to the object you are formatting)
☐ Click **Format** on the menu bar, then click **Selected** *Object*, or right-click the object, then click **Format** *Object*
☐ In the Format Object dialog box, select the appropriate options, then click **OK**

Mouse Method

☐ Double-click the appropriate chart object to select it

☐ In the Format Object dialog box, select the appropriate options, then click **OK**

ALIGN TEXT AND GRAPHICS

Menu Method

☐ Click the graphic to select it, click **Format** on the menu bar, then click **Object** (in the following steps, *Object* refers to the object you are formatting)

☐ In the Format *Object* dialog box, click the **Layout tab** if necessary, then click **Advanced**

☐ In the Advanced Layout dialog box, click the **Text Wrapping tab** if necessary, select the appropriate style, then click **OK**

☐ In the Format *Object* dialog box, click **OK**

Button Method

☐ Click the graphic to select it

☐ Click the **Text Wrapping button** 🖾 on the Picture toolbar

☐ Click the appropriate option from the menu

WORD SKILL SET 11: CUSTOMIZING WORD

CREATE, EDIT, AND RUN MACROS

Create Macros

Menu Method

- ☐ Click **Tools** on the menu bar, point to **Macro**, then click **Record New Macro**
- ☐ In the Record Macro dialog box, type the macro name in the Macro name text box
- ☐ Click the **Store macro in list arrow**, then click the appropriate macro storage option
- ☐ To assign a keyboard shortcut to the macro, click the **Keyboard button**, in the Customize Keyboard dialog box, press the appropriate keyboard shortcut to insert a shortcut key in the Press new shortcut key text box, click **Assign**, then click **Close**
- ☐ To assign a button to the macro, click the **Toolbar button** to open the Customize dialog box, click the **Commands tab**, select the appropriate command in the Commands section, drag it to the toolbar or to a menu, then click **Close**
- ☐ Perform the actions for the macro
- ☐ Click **Tools** on the menu bar, point to **Macro**, then click **Stop Recording**

Button Method

- ☐ Click the **Record Macro button** 🔘 on the Visual Basic toolbar
- ☐ Follow the second through sixth bullets in the Create Macros Menu Method above
- ☐ Click the **Stop Recording button** 🔳 on the Stop Recording toolbar

Run Macros

Menu Method

- ☐ Click **Tools** on the menu bar, then click **Options**
- ☐ In the Options dialog box, click the **Security tab**, then click **Macro Security**
- ☐ In the Security dialog box, make sure the **Security Level tab** is selected, click the **Medium option button** or the **Low option button**, click **OK** in the Security dialog box, then click **OK** in the Options dialog box
- ☐ Open the file that contains the macro, clicking **Yes** to enable a macro if prompted
- ☐ Click **Tools** on the menu bar, point to **Macro**, then click **Macros**
- ☐ In the Macros dialog box, make sure the appropriate macro is selected in the macro list, then click **Run**

Button Method

- ☐ Follow the first through fourth bullets in the Run Macros Menu Method above
- ☐ Click the button on the toolbar for the macro you created

Keyboard Method

☐ Follow the first through fourth bullets in the Run Macros Menu Method above

☐ Press the keyboard combination for the macro you created

Edit Macros

Menu Method

☐ Click **Tools** on the menu bar, point to **Macro**, then click **Macros**

☐ In the the Macros dialog box, make sure the appropriate macro is selected in the macro list, then click **Edit**

☐ In the Microsoft Visual Basic Editor window, make the appropriate modifications

☐ Click **File** on the menu bar, then click **Close and Return to Microsoft Word**

CUSTOMIZE MENUS AND TOOLBARS

Create Menus

Menu Method

☐ Click **Tools** on the menu bar, then click **Customize**, or right-click any toolbar, then click **Customize** on the shortcut menu

☐ In the Customize dialog box, click the **Commands tab**, click the **Save in list arrow**, then click the appropriate option

☐ Click **New Menu** in the Categories list box, then drag the **New Menu command** from the Commands list to the menu bar and position it using 🅡⊞

☐ Click the appropriate option in the Categories list box, then drag the appropriate command on top of New Menu on the menu bar so that 🅡⊞ appears below New Menu, then release the mouse button when the pointer is in the box that appears below New Menu

☐ Right-click **New Menu** on the menu bar, select all of the text in the Name box on the shortcut menu, then type the **menu name**

☐ Click anywhere in the document to close the shortcut menu, then click **Close** in the Customize dialog box

Create Toolbars

Menu Method

☐ Click **Tools** on the menu bar, then click **Customize** or right-click a toolbar, then click **Customize** on the shortcut menu

☐ In the Customize dialog box, click the **Toolbars tab**, then click **New**

☐ In the New Toolbar dialog box, type the toolbar name in the Toolbar name text box, click the **Make toolbar available to list arrow**, click the appropriate option, then click **OK**

☐ Click the **Commands tab**, then click the appropriate option in the Categories list box

☐ Drag the appropriate command(s) from the Commands list box to the new toolbar, then release the mouse button when 🅡⊞ is positioned on the toolbar

☐ Click **Close** in the Customize dialog box

Add Buttons to Toolbars

Menu Method

☐ Click **Tools** on the menu bar, then click **Customize** or right-click a tool-bar, then click **Customize** on the shortcut menu

☐ In the Customize dialog box, click the **Commands tab**, click the **Save in list arrow**, then click the appropriate option

☐ Click the appropriate option in the Categories list box, drag the appropriate command to the appropriate location on the appropriate toolbar, then release the mouse button when the ⬚ pointer is on the toolbar

☐ Click **Close** in the Customize dialog box

Remove Buttons from Toolbars

Button Method

☐ Click the **Toolbar options button** ⬚ on the toolbar from which you want to delete a button, point to **Add or Remove Buttons**, then point to the **toolbar name**

☐ Click the **button** on the shortcut menu you want to delete so that it no longer has a checkmark next to it

Keyboard Method

☐ Press and hold **[Alt]**

☐ Click the button you want to remove, then drag it off of the toolbar

Skill Set 12: Workgroup Collaboration

Track, Accept, and Reject Changes to Documents

Track Changes

Menu Method

☐ Click **Tools** on the menu bar, then click **Track Changes**
☐ Make text and formatting changes

Menu Method

☐ Click the **Track Changes button** 🔲 on the Reviewing toolbar
☐ Make text and formatting changes

Review Changes

Button Method

☐ In Normal view, position the insertion point over the marked change or text in brackets to see the registered user's name and the current date appear in a ScreenTip, along with a brief description of the change
☐ Click the appropriate button on the Reviewing toolbar to navigate through and display changes and comments, using Table WD-25 as a reference

OR

☐ In Print Layout view, position the insertion point over the ScreenTip in the right margin to see the registered user's name and the date the change or comment was made
☐ Click the appropriate button on the Reviewing toolbar to navigate through and display changes and comments, using Table WD-25 as a reference

Table WD-25 Reviewing Toolbar Navigation Buttons

Button	Effect
Next button 🔲	Move to the next comment or change
Previous button 🔲	Move to the previous comment or change
Show button 🔲 Show ▾	Can change display options: comments, text insertions and deletions, formatting changes, select reviewers to display, and display the reviewing pane at the bottom of the window

Respond to Changes

Menu Method

☐ Right-click the change to which you want to respond
☐ Click **Accept Deletion** or **Reject Deletion** on the shortcut menu as appropriate

Button Method

☐ Select the change to which you want to respond, then click the appropriate button on the Reviewing toolbar, using Table WD-26 as a reference

Table WD-26 Reviewing Toolbar Response Buttons

Button	Use
Accept Change button 🔊	To accept a change
Accept Change list arrow 🔊▾	To choose to accept a change, all changes, or all shown changes
Reject Change/Delete Comment button 🔊	To reject a change or delete a comment
Reject Change/Delete Comment list arrow 🔊▾	To choose to reject the change or delete the comment; to reject all changes; or to delete all comments
New Comment button 🔒	To insert a new comment

MERGE INPUT FROM SEVERAL REVIEWERS

Distribute Documents for Review via E-mail

Menu Method

☐ Make sure you are connected to the Internet
☐ Click **File** on the menu bar, point to **Send To**, then click **Mail Recipient (for Review)** or **Mail Recipient (as Attachment)** to open your e-mail program's program window, displaying an e-mail message with an attachment consisting of the the document currently open in Word
☐ In the e-mail message, type the e-mail address in the **To text box**, then click the **Send button**

Merge Revisions

Menu Method

☐ Open the revised document
☐ Click **Tools** on the menu bar, then click **Compare and Merge Documents**
☐ In the Compare and Merge Documents dialog box, navigate to the appropriate drive and folder, click the original document, then click **Merge**

INSERT AND MODIFY HYPERLINKS TO OTHER DOCUMENTS AND WEB PAGES

Insert Hyperlinks to Another Place in the Document

Menu Method

☐ Select the text you want to become a hyperlink
☐ Click **Insert** on the menu bar, then click **Hyperlink** or right-click, then click **Hyperlink** on the shortcut menu

☐ In the Insert Hyperlink dialog box, click **Place in This Document** in the Link to section, select a location in the Select a place in this document list, then click **OK**

Button Method

☐ Select the text you want to become a hyperlink
☐ Click the **Insert Hyperlink button** 🔗 on the Standard Buttons toolbar
☐ In the Insert Hyperlink dialog box, click **Place in This Document** in the Link to section, select a location in the Select a place in this document list, then click **OK**

Keyboard Method

☐ Select the text you want to become a hyperlink
☐ Press **[Ctrl][K]**
☐ In the Insert Hyperlink dialog box, click **Place in This Document** under Link to on the left, select a location in the Select a place in this document list, then click **OK**

Insert Hyperlinks to Another Document

Menu Method

☐ Select the text you want to become a hyperlink
☐ Click **Insert** on the menu bar, then click **Hyperlink** or right-click, then click **Hyperlink** on the shortcut menu
☐ In the Insert Hyperlink dialog box, click **Existing File or Web Page** in the Link to section, click the **Look in list arrow**, navigate to the appropriate drive and folder, click the filename in the list, then click **OK**

Button Method

☐ Select the text you want to become a hyperlink
☐ Click the **Insert Hyperlink button** 🔗 on the Standard Buttons toolbar
☐ In the Insert Hyperlink dialog box, click **Existing File or Web Page** in the Link to section, click the **Look in list arrow**, navigate to the appropriate drive and folder, click the filename in the list, then click **OK**

Keyboard Method

☐ Select the text you want to become a hyperlink
☐ Press **[Ctrl][K]**
☐ In the Insert Hyperlink dialog box, click **Existing File or Web Page** in the Link to section, click the **Look in list arrow**, navigate to the appropriate drive and folder, click the filename in the list, then click **OK**

Insert Hyperlinks to Web Pages

Menu Method

☐ Make sure you are connected to the Internet
☐ Select the text you want to become a hyperlink
☐ Click **Insert** on the menu bar, then click **Hyperlink** or right-click, then click **Hyperlink** on the shortcut menu
☐ In the Insert Hyperlink dialog box, click **Existing File or Web Page** in the Link to section of your Web browser
☐ Click the **Address text box**, then type the URL
☐ Click **OK**

Button Method

☐ Make sure you are connected to the Internet
☐ Select the text you want to become a hyperlink
☐ Click the **Insert Hyperlink button** 🔗 on the Standard Buttons toolbar
☐ Follow the fourth through sixth bullets in the Insert Hyperlinks to Web Pages Menu Method above

Keyboard Method

☐ Make sure you are connected to the Internet
☐ Select the text you want to become a hyperlink
☐ Press **[Ctrl][K]**
☐ Follow the fourth through sixth bullets in the Insert Hyperlinks to Web Pages Menu Method above

OR

☐ Click where you want the hyperlink to the URL to appear
☐ Type the URL of the Web page to which you want to link, then press **[Enter]** or **[Spacebar]** to automatically convert the text to a hyperlink to that Web address

Modify Hyperlinks

Menu Method

☐ Right-click the hyperlink, then click **Edit Hyperlink** on the shortcut menu
☐ In the Edit Hyperlink dialog box, make the appropriate modifications, then click **OK**

OR

☐ Right-click the hyperlink, then click **Remove Hyperlink** on the short-cut menu

---

CREATE AND EDIT WEB DOCUMENTS IN WORD

Create a Web Document in Word

Menu Method

☐ Click **File** on the menu bar, click **New** to open the New Document task pane, click the **General Templates link** in the task pane to open the Templates dialog box, then click the **Web Pages tab**
☐ Click the **Web Page Wizard icon**, then click **OK** to start the Web Page Wizard
☐ Navigate through the Web Page Wizard, making changes or accepting the defaults as appropriate to create the Web page, then click **Finish**

Open and Edit Web Documents in Word

Menu Method

☐ Click **File** on the menu bar, then click **Open**
☐ In the Open dialog box, navigate to the appropriate drive and folder, make sure the Files of type box lists **All Word Documents**, click the HTML file, then click **Open**
☐ Edit the document by adding, deleting, and modifying graphics, text, frames, and URLs

Save Word Documents to the Web

Menu Method

☐ Make sure that you are connected to the Internet
☐ Click **File** on the menu bar, then click **Save as Web Page**
☐ In the Save As dialog box, click **My Network Places** under Save in
☐ If a Web server is listed in the dialog box, and if you have permission to post files to it, double-click it; if no Web server is listed, double-click **Add Network Place**, navigate through the Add Network Place, then click **Finish**, or navigate to the appropriate drive and folder
☐ Type the filename in the File name box, then click **Save**

CREATE DOCUMENT VERSIONS

Menu Method

☐ Click **File** on the menu bar, then click **Versions**
☐ In the Versions dialog box, click **Save Now**
☐ In the Save Version dialog box, type any comments in the Comments on version text box, then click **OK**
☐ In the Save As dialog box, type the filename in the File name text box, then click **Save**

PROTECT DOCUMENTS

Menu Method

☐ Click **Tools** on the menu bar, then click **Protect Document**
☐ In the Protect Document dialog box, select the appropriate option button, type the **password** in the Password (optional) text box if necessary, then click **OK**
☐ If necessary, type the **password** again in the Confirm Password dialog box, then click **OK**

DEFINE AND MODIFY DEFAULT FILE LOCATIONS FOR WORKGROUP TEMPLATES

Menu Method

Note: These steps should only be performed if you want to permanently change the default location for workgroup templates and permanently add additional tabs to the Templates dialog box.

☐ Click **Tools** on the menu bar, then click **Options**
☐ In the Options dialog box, click the **File Locations tab**, click **Workgroup templates** in the File types list, then click **Modify**
☐ In the Modify Location dialog box, select the folder or drive in the Look in list box at the top of the dialog box you want to be the location listed for workgroup templates on the File Locations tab, then click **OK**
☐ Click **OK** in the Options dialog box

MODIFY AND RE-POST HTML DOCUMENTS

Menu Method

☐ Make sure you are connected to the Internet
☐ Start Internet Explorer
☐ Click **File** on the menu bar, then click **Open**
☐ In the Open dialog box, click **Browse**
☐ In the Microsoft Internet Explorer dialog box, navigate to the appropriate drive and folder, click the HTML file, click **Open**, then click **OK** in the Open dialog box
☐ Click **File** on the menu bar, then click **Edit with Microsoft Word** to open the HTML file in Word
☐ Make the appropriate modifications, click **File** on the menu bar, then click **Save As**
☐ In the Save As dialog box, click **My Network Places** on the Places bar
☐ If a Web server is listed in the dialog box, and if you have permission to post files to it, double-click it, if no Web server is listed, double-click **Add Network Place**, navigate through the Add Network Place, then click **Finish**, or navigate to the appropriate drive and folder
☐ Click **Save**

ATTACH DIGITAL SIGNATURES TO DOCUMENTS

Attach Digital Signatures

Menu Method

☐ Click **Tools** on the menu bar, then click **Options**
☐ In the Options dialog box, click the **Security tab**, then click **Digital Signatures**
☐ In the Digital Signature dialog box, click **Add**, then click **OK** or **Yes** in any message boxes
☐ In the Select Certificate dialog box, make sure the registered user's name is listed and selected, then click **View Certificate**
☐ Click **OK** in the Certificate dialog box, then click **OK** in the Select Certificate dialog box
☐ Click **OK** in the Digital Signature dialog box, then click **OK** in the Options dialog box

Use Digital Signatures to Authenticate Documents

Menu Method

☐ Click **Tools** on the menu bar, then click **Options**
☐ In the Options dialog box, click the **Security tab**, then click **Digital Signatures**
☐ In the Digital Signature dialog box, make sure the correct certificate is selected, then click **View Certificate**
☐ Note the names next to Issued to and Issued by, then make sure the certificate is still valid
☐ Click **OK** in the Certificate dialog box, click **OK** in the Digital Signature dialog box, then click **OK** in the Options dialog box

WORD SKILL SET 13: USING MAIL MERGE

MERGE LETTERS WITH A WORD, EXCEL, OR ACCESS DATA SOURCE

Menu Method

- ☐ Click **Tools** on the menu bar, point to **Letters and Mailings**, then click **Mail Merge Wizard**
- ☐ Make sure the **Letters option button** is selected in the Mail Merge task pane, click the **Next: Starting document link** at the bottom of the task pane, make sure the **Use the current document option button** is selected, then click the **Next: Select recipients link**
- ☐ Make sure the **Use an existing list option button** is selected, then click the **Browse link**
- ☐ In the Select Data Source dialog box, navigate to the appropriate drive and folder, click the data source, then click **Open**
- ☐ If the Select Table dialog box opens, click the table or query, then click **OK**
- ☐ In the Mail Merge Recipients dialog box, click **OK**
- ☐ Navigate through the rest of the Mail Merge task pane, making changes or accepting the defaults as appropriate to create the mail merge

MERGE LABELS WITH A WORD, EXCEL, OR ACCESS DATA SOURCE

Menu Method

- ☐ Create a new blank document
- ☐ Click **Tools** on the menu bar, point to **Letters and Mailings**, then click **Mail Merge Wizard**
- ☐ In the Mail Merge task pane, click the **Labels option button**, click the **Next: Starting document link**, make sure the **Change document layout option button** is selected, then click the **Label options link**
- ☐ In the Label Options dialog box, click the appopriate options, then click **OK**
- ☐ Make sure the **Use the current document option button** is selected, then click the **Next: Select recipients link**
- ☐ Make sure the **Use an existing list option button** is selected, then click the **Browse link**
- ☐ In the Select Data Source dialog box, navigate to the appropriate drive and folder, click the data source, then click **Open**
- ☐ If the Select Table dialog box opens, click the table or query, then click **OK**
- ☐ In the Mail Merge Recipients dialog box, click **OK**
- ☐ Navigate through the rest of the Mail Merge task pane, making changes or accepting the defaults as appropriate to create the labels

USE OUTLOOK DATA AS A MAIL MERGE DATA SOURCE

Menu Method

Note: Outlook must be set as your default mail client in order to use it as a data source. Open Outlook, click Tools on the menu bar, then click Options. In the Options dialog box, click the Other tab if necessary, then click the Make Outlook the default program for E-mail, Contacts and Calendar check box, if necessary.

- ☐ Click **Tools** on the menu bar, point to **Letters and Mailings**, then click **Mail Merge Wizard**
- ☐ In the Mail Merge task pane, select a document type, click the **Next: Starting document link**, select the appropriate options, then click the **Next: Select recipients link**
- ☐ Click the **Select from Outlook contacts option button**, then click the **Choose Contacts Folder link**
- ☐ In the Select Contacts List folder dialog box, make sure **Contacts** is selected in the list, then click **OK**
- ☐ In the Mail Merge Recipients dialog box, click **Clear All**, click the appropriate check boxes, then click **OK**
- ☐ Navigate through the rest of the Mail Merge task pane, making changes or accepting the defaults as appropriate to create the mail merge

MICROSOFT EXCEL 2002
EXAM REFERENCE

Getting Started with Excel 2002

The Excel MOUS exams assume a basic level of proficiency in Excel. This section is intended to help you reference these basic skills while you are preparing to take the Excel Core or Expert exams.

☐ Starting and exiting Excel
☐ Viewing the Excel window
☐ Using toolbars
☐ Using task panes
☐ Opening and closing Excel workbooks
☐ Saving an Excel workbook
☐ Navigating in an Excel workbook
☐ Using views
☐ Using smart tags
☐ Getting Help

START AND EXIT EXCEL

Start Excel

Button Method

☐ Click the **Start button** [Start] on the Windows taskbar
☐ Point to **Programs**
☐ Click **Microsoft Excel**

OR

☐ Double-click the **Microsoft Excel program icon** [icon] on the desktop

Exit Excel

Menu Method

☐ Click **File** on the menu bar, then click **Exit**

Button Method

☐ Click the **Close button** [X] on the program window title bar

VIEW THE EXCEL WINDOW

Figure EX-1   Excel Window

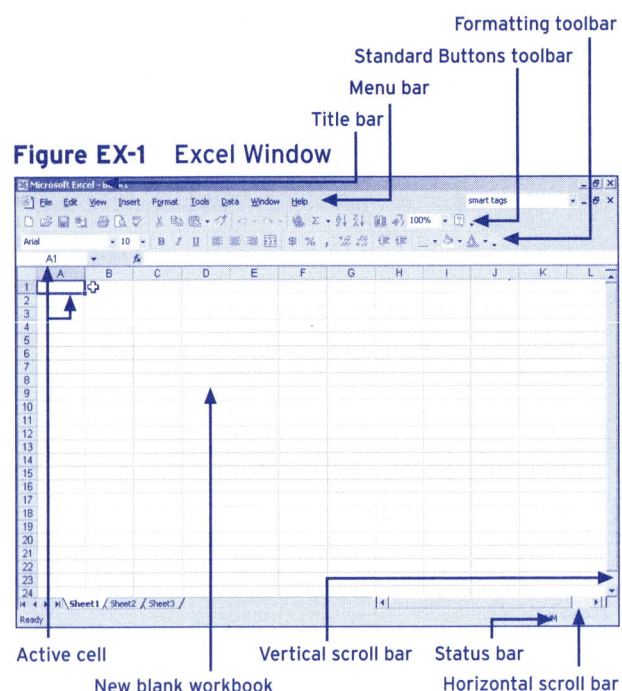

Formatting toolbar

Standard Buttons toolbar

Menu bar

Title bar

Active cell

New blank workbook

Vertical scroll bar

Status bar

Horizontal scroll bar

USE TOOLBARS

Display Toolbars

Menu Method

☐ Click **View** on the menu bar, point to **Toolbars**, then click the toolbar you want to display

OR

☐ Right-click any toolbar, then click the toolbar you want to display on the shortcut menu

Customize Toolbars

Menu Method

☐ Click **Tools** on the menu bar, then click **Customize**, or click **View** on the menu bar, point to **Toolbars**, then click **Customize**, or right-click any toolbar, then click **Customize** on the shortcut menu

☐ In the Customize dialog box, select the appropriate options, then click **Close**

Button Method

□ Click the **Toolbar Options button** ⯈ on the toolbar to customize
□ Point to **Add or Remove buttons**, then click **Customize**
□ Click the appropriate options in the Customize dialog box, then click **Close**

Reposition Toolbars

Mouse Method

□ Position the pointer in any blank area of the toolbar (not over a button)
□ When the pointer changes to ↔, press and hold the mouse button
□ Drag the toolbar to the desired location, then release the mouse button

Use Task Panes

Menu Method

□ If the task pane is not open, click **View** on the menu bar, then click **Task Pane** or right-click a blank location on the toolbar, then click **Task Pane** on the shortcut menu
□ Click the **Other Task Panes list arrow** ⯆ on the task pane title bar, then click the appropriate task pane
□ Click the **Back button** ◆ or the **Next button** ◆ on the task pane title bar to navigate to previously displayed task panes
□ Click the **Close button** ✕ on the task pane title bar to close the task pane

---

OPEN AND CLOSE WORKBOOKS

Open a New Workbook

Menu Method

□ Click **File** on the menu bar, then click **New**
□ Click **Blank Workbook** under New in the New Workbook task pane

Button Method

□ Click the **New button** ▯ on the Standard Buttons toolbar

Keyboard Method

□ Press **[Ctrl][N]**

Open an Existing Workbook

Menu Method

□ Click **File** on the menu bar, then click **Open**
□ In the Open dialog box, navigate to the appropriate drive and folder
□ Click the file, then click **Open**

Task Pane Method

□ Click a workbook under the Open a workbook section in the New Workbook task pane

OR

□ Click **More workbooks** under the Open a workbook section, then follow the second and third bullets in the Open an Existing Workbook Menu Method above

Button Method

☐ Click the **Open button** 📂
☐ Follow the second and third bullets in the Open an Existing Workbook Menu Method above

Keyboard Method

☐ Press **[Ctrl][O]**
☐ Follow the second and third bullets in the Open an Existing Workbook Menu Method above

Close Workbooks

Menu Method

☐ Click **File** on the menu bar, then click **Close**
☐ If prompted to save the file, click **Yes** or **No** as appropriate

Button Method

☐ Click the **Close Window button** ☒ on the menu bar
☐ If prompted to save the file, click **Yes** or **No** as appropriate

Keyboard Method

☐ Press **[Ctrl][W]**
☐ If prompted to save the file, click **Yes** or **No** as appropriate

---

NAVIGATE IN THE WORKBOOK WINDOW

Menu Method

☐ Click **Edit** on the menu bar, then click **Go To**
☐ In the Go To dialog box, select the appropriate options, then click **OK**

Keyboard Method

☐ Press **[Ctrl][G]**
☐ Follow the steps in the second bullet of the Navigate in the Workbook Window Menu Method above
   OR
☐ Use Table EX-1 as a reference to navigate through the worksheet

Table EX-1: Navigation Keyboard Shortcuts

Key	Moves the insertion point
[Ctrl][Home]	To the beginning of the workbook (cell A1)
[Ctrl][End]	To the end of the workbook
[Page Up]	One screen up
[Page Down]	One screen down
[Alt][Page Up]	One screen to the left
[Alt][Page Down]	One screen to the right

Scroll Bar Method

☐ Drag the scroll box in the scroll bar to move within the workbook without moving the insertion point
☐ Click above the scroll box in the vertical scroll bar to jump up a screen
☐ Click below the scroll box in the vertical scroll bar to jump down a screen
☐ Click the **up scroll arrow** in the vertical scroll bar to move up one row
☐ Click the **down scroll arrow** in the vertical scroll bar to move down one row

SAVE AN EXISTING EXCEL WORKBOOK

Menu Method

☐ Click **File** on the menu bar, then click **Save**

Button Method

☐ Click the **Save button** 🔲 on the Standard Buttons toolbar

Keyboard Method

☐ Press **[Ctrl][S]**

USE VIEWS

Refer to Table EX-2 to change worksheet views.

Table EX-2: Workbook Views

View	What you see	Standard Buttons Toolbar	Menu Method Toolbar
Normal view	Formatted workbook, but not headers, footers, or some graphics; does not show workbook as it would appear when printed		Click View on the menu bar, then click Normal
Page Break Preview	Same as Normal view, except with blue lines indicating page breaks; page breaks can be manually modified by dragging ⤢ and ⬍		Click View on the menu bar, then click Page Break Preview
Print Preview	Workbook as it would appear when printed	Print Preview button 🔍	Click File on the menu bar, then click Print Preview
Zoom	Workbook magnified or reduced to see more or less	Zoom list arrow 100% ▼	Click View on the menu bar, click Zoom, in the Zoom dialog box make the selection, then click OK

USE SMART TAGS

Button Method

☐ Move the pointer over text underlined with a purple triangle in the corner until the **Smart Tag Actions button** ⓢ appears

☐ Click ⓢ to see the actions you can perform, then select an action

GET HELP

Menu Method

☐ Click **Help** on the menu bar, then click **Microsoft Excel Help**
☐ Use Table EX-3 as a reference to select the most appropriate way to search for help using the Microsoft Excel Help window

Button Method

☐ Click the **Microsoft Excel Help button** 🔲 on the Standard Buttons toolbar
☐ Use Table EX-3 as a reference to select the most appropriate way to search for help using the Microsoft Excel Help window

OR

☐ Click the **Ask a Question text box** [Type a question for help ▼] on the menu bar
☐ Type your question, then press **[Enter]**
☐ Select the option you want from the drop down list, then read about your question in the Microsoft Excel Help window, using Table EX-3 as a reference

Keyboard Method

☐ Press **[F1]**
☐ Use Table EX-3 as a reference to select the most appropriate way to search for help using the Microsoft Excel Help window

Table EX-3: Microsoft Help Window Tabs

Tab	To use
Contents	Click the Expand indicator ➕ next to each topic you want to explore further, then click the selection you want and read the results in the right pane
Answer Wizard	Type your question in the What would you like to do? text box, click Search, then read the results in the right pane
Index	Type the keyword(s) you want to search for in the Type keyword text box, click Search, then read the results in the right pane

EXCEL CORE EXAM REFERENCE

Skill Sets:
1 Working with cells and cell data
2 Managing workbooks
3 Formatting and printing worksheets
4 Modifying workbooks
5 Creating and revising formulas
6 Creating and modifying graphics
7 Workgroup collaboration

EXCEL SKILL SET 1: WORKING WITH CELLS AND CELL DATA

INSERT, DELETE, AND MOVE CELLS

Insert Cells

Menu Method

- ☐ Click where to insert cells
- ☐ Click **Insert** on the menu bar, then click **Cells**
- ☐ In the Insert dialog box, select the appropriate option button
- ☐ Click **OK**

  OR

- ☐ Right-click where to insert cells
- ☐ Click **Insert** on the shortcut menu
- ☐ If the Insert dialog box opens, select the appropriate option button, then click **OK**

Delete Cells

Menu Method

- ☐ Click the cell(s), row(s), or column(s) to delete
- ☐ Click **Edit** on the menu bar, then click **Delete**, or right-click, then click **Delete** on the shortcut menu
- ☐ If the Delete dialog box opens, select the appropriate option button, then click **OK**

Merge Cells

Menu Method

- ☐ Select the cells to merge, ensuring that no more than one cell in the range contains data or fomatting
- ☐ Click **Format** on the menu bar, then click **Cells**, or right-click, then click **Format Cells** on the shortcut menu
- ☐ In the Format Cells dialog box, click the **Alignment tab**
- ☐ Click the **Merge cells check box**, then click **OK**

Button Method

☐ Select the cells to merge, ensuring that no more than one cell in the range contains data or fomatting
☐ Click the **Merge and Center button** 🔳 on the Formatting toolbar
☐ Click **OK** if a message box appears regarding multiple data values

Keyboard Method

☐ Select the cells to merge, ensuring that no more than one cell in the range contains data or fomatting
☐ Press **[Ctrl][1]**
☐ Follow the third and fourth bullets in the Merge Cells Menu Method above

Split Cells

Menu Method

☐ Select the merged cells
☐ Click **Format** on the menu bar, then click **Cells**, or right-click, then click **Format Cells** on the shortcut menu
☐ In the Format Cells dialog box, click the **Alignment tab**
☐ Click the **Merge cells check box** to deselect it, then click **OK**

Button Method

☐ Select the merged cells
☐ Click the **Merge and Center button** 🔳 on the Formatting toolbar

Keyboard Method

☐ Select the merged cells
☐ Press **[Ctrl][1]**
☐ Follow the third and fourth bullets in the Split Cells Menu Method above

Move Cells

Menu Method

☐ Select the cell(s) to move
☐ Click **Edit** on the menu bar, then click **Cut**
☐ Click where to insert the cells
☐ Click **Edit** on the menu bar, then click **Paste**

Button Method

☐ Select the cell(s) to move
☐ Click the **Cut button** ✂ on the Standard Buttons toolbar
☐ Click where to insert the cells
☐ Click the **Paste button** 📋 on the Standard Buttons toolbar

Keyboard Method

☐ Select the cell(s) to move
☐ Press **[Ctrl][X]**
☐ Click where to insert the cells

Mouse Method

□ Select the cell(s) to move
□ Place the mouse pointer over the edge of the selected range until it becomes ⇞
□ Click and drag the range to the appropriate location, then release the mouse button

ENTER AND EDIT CELL DATA INCLUDING TEXT, NUMBERS, AND FORMULAS

Enter Text and Numbers

Method

□ Click the cell where you want to enter text
□ Type the appropriate text or number, then move to the next cell using Table EX-4 below as a reference

Table EX-4: Navigating a Worksheet

Action	To move in relation to currently selected cell
[Enter]	To the cell below
[↑], [↓], [←] or [→]	To the cell above, below, left or right
[Tab]	One cell to the right
[Shift][Tab]	One cell to the left

Edit Text and Numbers

Keyboard Method

□ Click the cell to edit
□ Click the Formula bar, then edit the contents in the formula bar, or press **[F2]**, then edit the cell contents directly in the cell
□ Press **[Backspace]** to delete a character to the left of the insertion point, or press **[Delete]** to delete a character to the right of the insertion point

Mouse Method

□ Double-click the cell to edit
□ Edit the cell contents directly in the cell
□ Press **[Backspace]** to delete a character to the left of the insertion point, or press **[Delete]** to delete a character to the right of the insertion point

Apply Formats

Menu Method

□ Select the cell(s) to format
□ Click **Format** on the menu bar, then click **Cells**, or right-click, then click **Format Cells** on the shortcut menu

☐ In the Format Cells dialog box, select the appropriate tab, then make the appropriate formatting selections, using Table EX-5 as a reference

Table EX-5: Applying Formats Using the Format Cells Dialog Box

Tab	Options
Number	Change to Currency, Date, or other common number formats
Alignment	**Text alignment** (select vertical or horizontal alignment options between cell borders) **Text control** (text wrapping, shrink text to fit cell size, or merge cells) **Right-to-left** and **Orientation** (select text direction)
Font	**Font** (change font type) **Font style** (change to Regular, Bold, Italic, or Bold/Italic) **Size** (change font size) **Underline** (select text underlining options) **Color** (change font color) **Effects** (change to strikethrough, superscript, or subscript)
Border	Add borders on selected cell edges
Patterns	Fill cell(s) with color or patterns

Button Method

☐ Select the cell(s) to format
☐ Use the buttons on the Formatting toolbar to apply the appropriate format using Table EX-6 as a reference

Keyboard Method

☐ Select the cell(s) to format
☐ Press **[Ctrl[B]** to apply bold, press **[Ctrl][I]** to apply italics, or press **[Ctrl][U]** to apply underline format

Table EX-6: Applying Formats Using the Formatting toolbar

Button	Formatting	Effect
Arial	Font	Changes font style
10	Font Size	Changes font size
B	Bold	**Bold**
I	Italic	*Italic*
U	Underline	Underline
	Align Left	Aligns to the left cell edge
	Center	Aligns between left and right cell edges
	Align Right	Aligns to the right cell edge
	Merge and Center	Centers text across several cells
$	Currency Style	$1.23
%	Percent Style	123%
,	Comma Style	1.23
	Increase Decimal	1.230
	Decrease Decimal	1.2
	Decrease Indent	Decreases indentation from the left cell edge
	Increase Indent	Indents from the left cell edge
	Borders	Adds borders on selected cell edges
	Fill Color	Fills cell(s) with color
A	Font Color	Changes font color

Clear Cell Contents

Menu Method

☐ Click the cell(s) whose contents you want to clear

☐ Click **Edit** on the menu bar, point to **Clear**, then click **Contents**

OR

☐ Right-click, then click **Clear Contents** on the shortcut menu

Keyboard Method

☐ Select the cell(s) whose contents you want to clear

☐ Press **[Delete]**

Create Formulas

Button Method

☐ Click the cell where you want the formula to appear
☐ Type **=** (equals sign) to indicate the beginning of a formula, then type the rest of the formula using Table EX-7 as a reference
☐ Click the **Enter button** ☑ on the Formula bar

Keyboard Method

☐ Follow the first and second bullets in the Create Formulas Button Method above
☐ Press **[Enter]** or **[Tab]**

Table EX-7: Arithmetic Formula Operators

Operation	Operator	Example
Addition	+	=A3+5 (the contents of cell A3, plus 5)
Subtraction or Negation	–	=C2-C5 (the contents of cell C2, minus the contents of cell C5)
Multiplication	*	=B10*25 (25 times the contents of cell B10)
Division	/	=B7/4 (the contents of cell B7, divided by 4)

Add Functions to Formulas

Menu Method

☐ Click the cell where you want the formula to appear
☐ Type **=** (equals sign) to indicate the beginning of a formula, then start to type the formula
☐ At the appropriate point in the formula, click **Insert** on the menu bar, then click **Function**
☐ In the Insert Function dialog box, click the appropriate option(s), then click **OK**
☐ In the Function Arguments dialog box, click the appropriate option(s)
☐ If arguments are required for the function, select the cell(s) to which to apply the function in the worksheet
☐ Click **OK**

Button Method

☐ Follow the first and second bullets in the Add Functions to Formulas Menu Method above
☐ At the appropriate point in the in the formula, click the **Insert Function button** ☑ on the Formula bar
☐ Follow the fourth through sixth bullets in the Add Functions to Formulas Menu Method above

CHECK SPELLING

Check Worksheet Spelling

Menu Method

- ☐ Click **Tools** on the menu bar, then click **Spelling**
- ☐ In the Spelling dialog box click the appropriate options
- ☐ Click **Yes** to continue to check spelling at the beginning of the worksheet if necessary
- ☐ Click **OK** in the message box when the spelling check is complete

Button Method

- ☐ Click the **Spelling button** 📝 on the Standard Buttons toolbar
- ☐ Follow the second through fourth bullets in the Check Worksheet Spelling Menu Method above

Keyboard Method

- ☐ Press **[F7]**
- ☐ Follow the second through fourth bullets in the Check Worksheet Spelling Menu Method above

FIND AND REPLACE CELL DATA AND FORMATS

Use Find and Replace

Menu Method

- ☐ Click **Edit** on the menu bar, click **Replace**, then click the **Replace tab** in the Find and Replace dialog box if necessary
- ☐ Enter the text, formula, or value you wish to locate in the Find what text box, then press **[Tab]**
- ☐ Enter the text, formula, or value you wish to serve as replacement in the Replace with text box
- ☐ Click **Find Next** and **Replace** to locate all of the instances, selecting to either replace or skip the instance, then click **Close**

Keyboard Method

- ☐ Press **[Ctrl][F]** to open the Find dialog box, then click the **Replace tab**, or press **[Ctrl][H]**
- ☐ Follow the second through fourth bullets in the Use Find and Replace Menu Method above

Go to a Specific Cell

Menu Method

- ☐ Click **Edit** on the menu bar, then click **Go To**
- ☐ In the Go To dialog box, click the **Reference text box**, then type the appropriate cell reference
- ☐ Click **OK**

Keyboard Method

- [ ] Press **[Ctrl][G]**
- [ ] Follow the second and third bullet in the Go to a Specific Cell Menu Method above

Use Find and Replace to Change Cell Formats

Menu Method

- [ ] Click **Edit** on the menu bar, then click **Replace**
- [ ] In the Find and Replace dialog box, click **Options**
- [ ] Enter the text, formula, or value you wish to locate in the Find what text box, then click **Format**
- [ ] In the Find Format dialog box, select the appropriate options, then click **OK**
- [ ] Enter the text, formula, or value you wish to serve as replacement in the Replace with text box, then click **Format**
- [ ] In the Replace Format dialog box, select the appropriate options, then click **OK**
- [ ] Click **Find Next** and **Replace** to locate all of the instances, selecting to either replace or skip the instance, then click **Close**

Keyboard Method

- [ ] Press **[Ctrl][H]**
- [ ] Follow the second through sixth bullets in the Use Find and Replace to Change Cell Formats Menu Method above

WORK WITH A SUBSET OF DATA BY FILTERING LISTS

Filter Lists Using AutoFilter

Menu Method

- [ ] Click any cell in the list or range to filter
- [ ] Click **Data** on the menu bar, point to **Filter**, then click **AutoFilter**
- [ ] Click the **list arrow** of the column you wish to sort by first, then click the value by which to sort

Excel Skill Set 2: Managing Workbooks

Manage Workbook Files and Folders

Locate and Open Existing Workbooks

Menu Method

- ☐ Click **File** on the menu bar, then click **Open**
- ☐ In the Open dialog box, click the **Look in list arrow**
- ☐ Navigate to the appropriate drive and folder
- ☐ Click the file to open, then click **Open**

Button Method

- ☐ Click the **Open button** 📂 on the Standard Buttons toolbar
- ☐ Follow the second through fourth bullets in the Locate and Open Existing Workbooks Menu Method above

Keyboard Method

- ☐ Press **[Ctrl][O]**
- ☐ Follow the second through fourth bullets in the Locate and Open Existing Workbooks Menu Method above

Create Folders for Saving Workbooks

Menu Method

- ☐ Click **File** on the menu bar, then click **Save As**
- ☐ In the Save As dialog box, click the **Save in list arrow**, then navigate to the appropriate drive and folder
- ☐ Click the **Create New Folder button** 📁
- ☐ In the New Folder dialog box, type the name of the new folder, then click **OK**
- ☐ Type the name of the file in the File name text box, then click **Save**

Create Workbooks Using Templates

Menu Method

- ☐ Click **File** on the menu bar, then click **New**
- ☐ In the New Workbook task pane, click **General Templates** in the New from template section
- ☐ In the Templates dialog box, click the appropriate options, then click **OK**

SAVE WORKBOOKS USING DIFFERENT NAMES AND FILE FORMATS

Open a Workbook from a Folder Created for Workbook Storage

Menu Method

- ☐ Click **File** on the menu bar, then click **Open**
- ☐ In the Open dialog box, click the **Look in list arrow**
- ☐ Navigate to the appropriate drive and folder
- ☐ Click the file to open, then click **Open**

Button Method

- ☐ Click the **Open button** 📂 on the Standard Buttons toolbar
- ☐ Follow the second through fourth bullets in the Open a Workbook from a Folder Created for Workbook Storage Menu Method above

Keyboard Method

- ☐ Press **[Ctrl][O]**
- ☐ Follow the second through fourth bullets in the Open a Workbook from a Folder Created for Workbook Storage Menu Method above

Use Save As to Store Workbooks Using Different Names and in Different Locations

Menu Method

- ☐ Click **File** on the menu bar, then click **Save As**
- ☐ In the Save As dialog box, click the **Save in list arrow**, then navigate to the appropriate drive and folder
- ☐ Type the filename in the File name text box, then click **Save**

Use Save As to Store Workbooks in Different File Formats

Menu Method

- ☐ Click **File** on the menu bar, then click **Save As** to open the Save As dialog box
- ☐ In the File name text box, change the filename, click the **Save as type list arrow**, then select the appropriate file format
- ☐ Click **Save**
- ☐ If necessary, click **Yes** in the message box warning that some features may be lost

EXCEL SKILL SET 3: FORMATTING AND PRINTING WORKSHEETS

APPLY AND MODIFY CELL FORMATS

Format Cells with Type Styles and Fonts

Menu Method

☐ Select the cell(s) to format
☐ Click **Format** on the menu bar, then click **Style**
☐ In the Style dialog box, click the appropriate options, then click **OK**

Format Cells with Borders and Fills

Menu Method

☐ Select the cell(s) to format
☐ Click **Format** on the menu bar, then click **Cells**, or right-click, then click **Format Cells**
☐ In the Format Cells dialog box, click the **Border tab** or the **Patterns tab**
☐ Make the appropriate selections, then click **OK**

Button Method

☐ Select the cell(s) to format
☐ Click the **Borders list arrow** ▦ ▾ on the Formatting toolbar, click the appropriate border option, then click outside the selected cell(s)
☐ Click the **Fill Color list arrow** 🎨 ▾ on the Formatting toolbar, click the appropriate color, then click outside the selected cell(s)

Keyboard Method

☐ Select the cell(s) to format
☐ Press **[Ctrl][1]**
☐ Follow the third and fourth bullets in the Format Cells with Borders and Fills Menu Method above

MODIFY ROW AND COLUMN SETTINGS

Insert Rows and Columns

Menu Method

☐ Select the column to the right of or the row below where you want the new column to appear
☐ Click **Insert** on the menu bar, then click **Rows** or **Columns**
OR
☐ Select the column to the right of or the row below where you want the new column to appear
☐ Right-click, then click **Insert** on the shortcut menu

Keyboard Method
☐ Select the column to the right of or the row below where you want the new column to appear
☐ Press **[Ctrl][Shift][+]**

Delete Rows and Columns

Menu Method
☐ Select the row(s) or column(s) to delete
☐ Click **Edit** on the menu bar, then click **Delete**

OR

☐ Select the column or row to delete
☐ Right-click, then click **Delete** on the shortcut menu

Keyboard Method
☐ Select the row(s) or column(s) to delete
☐ Press **[Ctrl][Shift][-]**

Hide Rows and Columns

Menu Method
☐ Click any cell in the row or column to hide
☐ Click **Format** on the menu bar, then point to **Column** or **Row**
☐ Click **Hide** on the submenu

OR

☐ Select the row or column to hide
☐ Right-click, then click **Hide** on the shortcut menu

Mouse Method
☐ Position ↔ in the row or column head, on the border of the row or column to hide
☐ Drag ↔ to the left to hide the column, or drag up to hide the row

Redisplay Rows and Columns

Menu Method
☐ Select both of the rows or columns on either side of the row or column to redisplay, or any two cells on either side of it
☐ Click **Format** on the menu bar, point to **Column** or **Row**, then click **Unhide**

OR

☐ Select the row or column to hide
☐ Right-click, then click **Unhide** on the shortcut menu

Mouse Method
☐ Select both of the rows or columns on either side of the row or column to redisplay, or any two cells on either side of it
☐ Position ↔ or ↕ in the row or column head, on the border of the hidden row or column
☐ Drag ↔ or ↕ to the right to redisplay the column, or down to redisplay the row

Freeze Rows and Columns

Menu Method

□ Click any cell in the row to the right or column below where to freeze

□ Click **Window** on the menu bar, then click **Freeze Panes**

Unfreeze Rows and Columns

Menu Method

□ Click **Window** on the menu bar, then click **Unfreeze Panes**

Modify Row Height

Menu Method

□ Select the row or click any cell in the row

□ Click **Format** on the menu bar, point to **Row**, then click **Height**

□ In the Row Height dialog box, type the height, then click **OK**

Mouse Method

□ Position the mouse pointer over the bottom of the **row header**, until the pointer becomes ✛

□ Drag downward to enlarge the row to the desired size, or drag upward to decrease the size

OR

□ Position the mouse pointer over the bottom of the **row header**, until the pointer becomes ✛

□ Double-click to automatically adjust the row height to the size of the cell contents

Modify Column Width

Menu Method

□ Select the column or click any cell in the column

□ Click **Format** on the menu bar, point to **Column**, then click **Width**

□ In the Column Width dialog box, type the column width, then click **OK**

Mouse Method

□ Move the mouse pointer over the right divider between the columns until the pointer becomes ↔

□ Drag the column divider to the right to increase or the left to decrease the size

OR

□ Move the mouse pointer over the divider between the columns until the pointer becomes ↔

□ Double-click to automatically adjust the column width to the size of the text

Modify Alignment

Menu Method

☐ Click the cell(s) to align
☐ Click **Format** on the menu bar, then click **Cells**, or right-click, then click **Format Cells** on the shortcut menu
☐ In the Format Cells dialog box, click the **Alignment tab**
☐ Under Text alignment, click the **Horizontal list arrow** or the **Vertical list arrow**, click the appropriate alignment, then click **OK**

Button Method

☐ Select the cell(s) to align
☐ Click the appropriate alignment button on the Formatting toolbar using Table EX-8 as a reference

Table EX-8: Alignment Buttons on the Formatting Toolbar

Formatting toolbar button	Effect
▤	Left align
▤	Right align
▤	Center align
▤	Increase Indent
▤	Decrease Indent

Keyboard Method

☐ Select the cell(s) to align
☐ Press **[Ctrl][1]**
☐ Follow the third and fourth bullets in the Modify Alignment Menu Method above

Apply Styles

Menu Method

☐ Select the cell(s) to which to apply the style
☐ Click **Format** on the menu bar, then click **Style**
☐ In the Style dialog box, click the **Style name list arrow**, click the appropriate style, then click **OK**

USE AUTOMATED TOOLS TO FORMAT WORKSHEETS

Apply AutoFormats to Worksheets

Menu Method

☐ Select the cell(s) to format
☐ Click **Format** on the menu bar, then click **AutoFormat**
☐ In the AutoFormat dialog box, click the appropriate format, then click **OK**

MODIFY PAGE SETUP OPTIONS FOR WORKSHEETS

Change Worksheet Orientation

Menu Method

☐ Click **File** on the menu bar, then click **Page Setup**
☐ In the Page Setup dialog box, click the **Page tab**, if necessary
☐ Under Orientation, click the appropriate option button, then click **OK**

Add Headers and Footers to Worksheets

Menu Method

☐ Click **View** on the menu bar, then click **Header and Footer**
☐ In the Page Setup dialog box, click the **Header** or **Footer list arrow** to select predefined headers or footers, or click **Custom Header** or **Custom Footer** to create your own header or footer, make the appropriate selections for the header or footer in the Header or Footer dialog box, then click **OK** to close the Header or Footer dialog box
☐ Click **OK** to close the Page Setup dialog box

Set Page Options for Printing

Menu Method

☐ Click **File** on the menu bar, then click **Page Setup**
☐ In the Page Setup dialog box, make the appropriate selections using Table EX-9 as a reference, then click **OK**

Table EX-9: Page Setup Dialog Box Tabs

Tab	Options
Page	**Page orientation** (landscape or portrait) **Scaling** (adjust to print to a certain percentage or page determination) **Paper size** (select letter, legal, or other size) **Print quality** (select draft, high, medium, or low quality)
Margins	**Margins** (adjust top, bottom, left, right, header, or footer margins) **Center on page** (horizontal or vertical centering)
Header/Footer	Select options for preset or create custom headers and footers
Sheet	**Print area** (select ranges or objects to print) **Print title** (select rows or columns to repeat on each page) **Print** (select printing options, such as gridlines, column heads, and more) **Page order** (select whether to print multi-page worksheets going from left-to-right or top-to-bottom)

PREVIEW AND PRINT WORKSHEETS AND WORKBOOKS

Set and Print Print Areas

Menu Method

- ☐ Select the cell(s) to print
- ☐ Click **File** on the menu bar, point to **Print Area**, click **Set Print Area**, then click outside the selected cell(s)
- ☐ Click the **Print Preview button** 🔍 on the Standard Buttons toolbar, click **Print** in the Print Preview window, then click **OK** in the Print dialog box

Preview and Print Non-Adjacent Selections of Worksheets in a Workbook

Menu Method

- ☐ Select the cells or ranges to print by pressing and holding down **[Ctrl]** while you click on each
- ☐ Click **File** on the menu bar, then click **Print**
- ☐ Under the Print what section, click the **Selection option button** to select it, then click **Preview**
- ☐ In the Print Preview window, click **Next** on the Print Preview toolbar if necessary to view the next page
- ☐ Click **Print** on the Print Preview toolbar, then click **OK**

  OR

- ☐ Select the first cell or range to print
- ☐ Click **File** on the menu bar, point to **Print Area**, click **Set Print Area**, then click outside the selected cell(s)
- ☐ Click **View** on the menu bar, then click **Page Break Preview**
- ☐ For each additional cell or range, select it, right-click, then click **Add to Print Area** from the shortcut menu
- ☐ Click **File** on the menu bar, then click **Print**
- ☐ Click **OK** in the Print dialog box

EXCEL SKILL SET 4: MODIFYING WORKBOOKS

INSERT AND DELETE WORKSHEETS

Insert a New Worksheet into a Workbook

Menu Method

- [ ] Click **Insert** on the menu bar, then click **Worksheet**
  OR
- [ ] Right-click the worksheet tab to the right of where you want the new one to appear
- [ ] Click **Insert** on the shortcut menu
- [ ] In the Insert dialog box, click the **General tab** if necessary
- [ ] Click the **Worksheet icon**, then click **OK**

Delete Worksheets from a Workbook

Menu Method

- [ ] Click the **sheet tab** of the worksheet to delete
- [ ] Click **Edit** on the menu bar, then click **Delete Sheet**, or right-click, then click **Delete** on the shortcut menu
- [ ] Click **Delete** in the message box if necessary

MODIFY WORKSHEET NAMES AND POSITIONS

Move Worksheets Within a Workbook

Menu Method

- [ ] Click **Edit** on the menu bar, then click **Move or Copy Sheet**, or right-click the **worksheet tab** of the worksheet to move, then click **Move or Copy** on the shortcut menu
- [ ] In the Move or Copy dialog box, make the appropriate selections, then click **OK**

Mouse Method

- [ ] Position the pointer over the tab to move
- [ ] Press and hold down the mouse button, then drag to the appropriate location
- [ ] Release the mouse button

Name Worksheets

Menu Method

- [ ] Click **Format** on the menu bar, point to **Sheet**, then click **Rename** to highlight the name of the active sheet
- [ ] Type the new name, then press **[Enter]** or click anywhere in the sheet
  OR
- [ ] Right-click the sheet tab, then click **Rename** on the shortcut menu to highlight the existing sheet name
- [ ] Type the new name, then press **[Enter]** or click anywhere in the sheet

Mouse Method

☐ Double-click the **sheet tab**
☐ Type the new name, then press **[Enter]** or click anywhere in the sheet

Shading Worksheet Tabs

Menu Method

☐ Click **Format** on the menu bar, point to **Sheet**, then click **Tab Color**
☐ In the Format Tab Color dialog box, make the appropriate selections, then click **OK**

OR

☐ Right-click the **sheet tab**
☐ Click **Tab Color** on the shortcut menu
☐ In the Format Tab Color dialog box, click the appropriate color, then click **OK**

USE 3-D REFERENCES

Create Formulas Using 3-D References to the Same Cell

To enter formulas using 3-D references to the same cell, follow the guidelines in Table EX-10.

Create Formulas Using 3-D References to Different Cells

To enter formulas using 3-D references to different cells, follow the guidelines in Table EX-10.

Table EX-10: 3-D Cell Reference Formula Operators

Operator	Definition	Function	Example
!	Separates the sheet name from the cell reference	To be used when referencing any value not in the current sheet	Sheet2!C2 Indicates that the value to be used in the formula is cell C2 from sheet 2
:	Indicates that the same cell in a range of sheets is to be used in the formula	To be used when referencing the same cell from different sheets	=AVERAGE(Sheet1:Sheet4!A5) Calculates the average value of cell A5 from sheets 1, 2, 3, and 4
,	Separates cell/sheet references in a formula	To be used when referencing different cells from different sheets	=SUM(Sheet1!A3,Sheet2!A5) Totals the values in cell A3 in sheet 1, and A5 in sheet 2

EXCEL SKILL SET 5: CREATING AND REVISING FORMULAS

CREATE AND REVISE FORMULAS

Create Formulas

Button Method

□ Click the appropriate cell, then click in the **Formula Bar** or type the formula directly into the cell
□ Type =, then type the formula, typing the cell address or clicking each cell to reference it in the formula
□ Click the **Enter button** ☑ on the Formula Bar

Keyboard Method

□ Follow the first and second bullet in the Create Formulas Button Method above
□ Press **[Enter]** or **[Tab]**

Edit Formulas Using the Formula Bar

Button Method

□ Click the appropriate cell, then click the **Formula Bar**
□ Modify the formula in the Formula Bar
□ Click the **Enter button** ☑ on the Formula Bar

Keyboard Method

□ Follow the first and second bullets in the Edit Formulas Using the Formula Bar Button Method above
□ Press **[Enter]** or **[Tab]**

Enter a Range in a Formula by Dragging

Keyboard Method

□ Click the appropriate cell
□ Type **=**, then start to type the formula
□ To enter a range, type **(**, click the first cell in the range, press and hold the mouse button, then drag to select the range
□ Type **)**
□ Press **[Enter]** or **[Tab]**

USE RELATIVE REFERENCES IN FORMULAS

Use Figure EX-2 as a reference for using relative and absolute references in formulas. To type a relative reference, click the cell or type the cell address in the formula to reference it.

Figure EX-2   Relative and Absolute Cell Reference

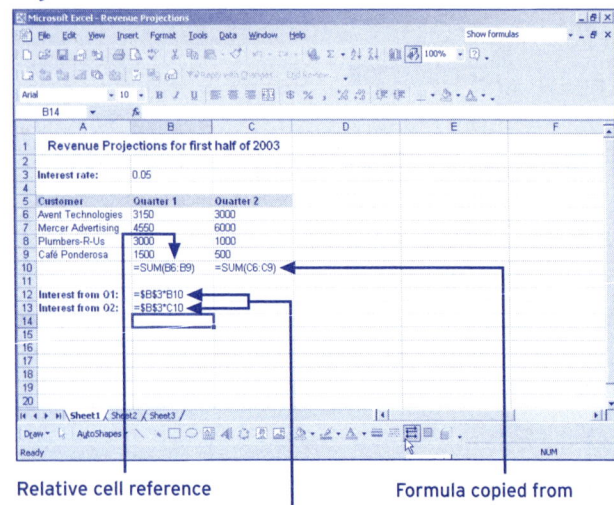

Relative cell reference

Absolute cell references

Formula copied from
cell B10 to cell C10; relative
cell reference has changed
to reflect column C

Use Absolute References in Formulas

Keyboard Method

☐ Click the appropriate cell, then click the **Formula Bar** or type the formula directly into the cell
☐ Select the cell reference in the Formula Bar for the cell you want to
make an absolute reference for
☐ Press **[F4]**, then verify that the cell reference now reads **A1** (where A1
is the cell address)
☐ Press **[Enter]** or **[Tab]**

USE STATISTICAL, DATE AND TIME, FINANCIAL, AND LOGICAL FUNCTIONS IN FORMULAS

Create a Formula Using a Function

Menu Method

☐ Click the appropriate cell
☐ Click **Insert** on the menu bar, then click **Function**
☐ In the Insert Function dialog box, select the appropriate function using
Table EX-11 as a reference, then click **OK**
☐ In the Function Argument dialog box, make the appropriate selections,
or select the appropriate cells if necessary, then click **OK**

Button Method

☐ Click the appropriate cell
☐ Click the **Insert Function button** 🔣 on the Formula Bar
☐ Follow the third and fourth bullets in the Create a Formula Using a Function Menu Method above

Table EX-11: Examples of Excel Functions

Function	Example	Calculates
SUM	=SUM(A4:C4)	The total of the values in cells A4, B4, and C4
MIN	=MIN(B10,B13,B15)	The lowest value in the cells B10, B13, and B15
MAX	=MAX(C14,C18:C20)	The highest value in the cells C14, C18, C19, and C20
PMT	= PMT(rate,nper,pv,fv,type)	Payment for a loan where **rate** is the interest rate, **Nper** is the number of payments, and **Pv** is the principal on the loan, **Fv** is the cash balance after the last payment (if omitted, is assumed to be zero), **Type** is the number 0 (zero) or 1 and indicates when payments are due
IF	=IF(logical_test,value_if_true,value_if_false)	Performs the logical test, then returns a value if it is true or false, such as whether a budget is within its limits

Excel Skill Set 6: Creating and Modifying Graphics

Create, Modify, Position, and Print Charts

Create a Chart

Menu Method

☐ Select the range you want to use to create a chart
☐ Click **Insert** on the menu bar, then click **Chart**
☐ Navigate through the Chart Wizard, using Table EX-12 as a reference to select the chart type, make changes or accept the defaults as appropriate to create the chart, then click **Finish**

Button Method

☐ Select the range you want to use to create a chart
☐ Click the **Chart Wizard button** 📊 on the Standard Buttons toolbar
☐ Follow the third bullet in the Create a Chart Menu Method above

Table EX-12: Common Chart Types

Chart type	Looks like	Could be used to
Column	📊	Show relative amounts for one or multiple values at different points in time (displays vertically)
Bar	📊	Show relative amounts for one or multiple values at different points in time (displays horizontally)
Line	📈	Show growth trends over time
Pie	🥧	Show proportions

Move a Chart

Menu Method

☐ Select the chart
☐ Click **Chart** on the menu bar, then click **Location**
☐ In the Chart Location dialog box, select the appropriate options, then click **OK**

Mouse Method

☐ Select the chart
☐ Move the pointer over the Chart Area section of the chart
☐ Press and hold the left mouse button, then drag the chart to the appropriate location using ✛

Resize a Chart

Mouse Method

- ☐ Select the chart
- ☐ Move the pointer over any sizing handle on the chart until it changes to the appropriate pointer, using Table EX-13 below as a reference
- ☐ Press and hold the left mouse button while you drag to resize the chart, then release the mouse button

Table EX-13: Resize Pointers

Pointer	Used to
↖ or ↗	Resize proportionally
↔	Resize horizontally
↕	Resize vertically

Change a Chart Type

Menu Method

- ☐ Select the chart
- ☐ Click **Chart** on the menu bar, then click **Chart Type**, or right-click, then click **Chart Type** on the shortcut menu
- ☐ In the Chart Type dialog box, make the appropriate selections, then click **OK**

Print Charts

Menu Method

- ☐ Select the chart
- ☐ Click **File** on the menu bar, then click **Print**
- ☐ Verify that the Selected Chart option button is selected under Print what
- ☐ Click **OK** in the Print dialog box

Button Method

- ☐ Select the chart
- ☐ Click the **Print button** 🖶 on the Standard Buttons toolbar

Keyboard Method

- ☐ Select the chart
- ☐ Press **[Ctrl][P]**
- ☐ Follow the third and fourth bullets in the Print Charts Menu Method above

Format Charts and Chart Text

Menu Method

☐ Click the appropriate chart object to select it (in the following steps, *object* refers to the object you are formatting)

☐ Click **Format** on the menu bar, then click **Selected** *Object*, or right-click the object, then click **Format** *Object* on the shortcut menu

☐ In the Format *Object* dialog box, select the appropriate options, then click **OK**

Button Method

☐ Click the appropriate chart object to select it (in the following steps, *object* refers to the object you are formatting)

☐ Click the **Format** *Object* **button** 📑 on the Chart toolbar

☐ In the Format *Object* dialog box, select the appropriate options, then click **OK**

Mouse Method

☐ Double-click the appropriate chart object to select it

☐ In the Format *Object* dialog box, select the appropriate options, then click **OK**

CREATE, MODIFY, AND POSITION GRAPHICS

Create Graphics

Button Method

☐ Click the appropriate graphics button on the Drawing toolbar, using Table EX-14 below as a reference, then draw the graphic using ╋.

Table EX-14: Drawing Toolbar Options

Button	Button Name	Used to
AutoShapes ▾	AutoShapes	Create shapes such as stars, hearts, and callouts
◥	Line	Create straight lines
◥	Arrow	Create arrows
▢	Rectangle	Create rectangles. Can also be used to create squares by pressing and holding [Shift] while dragging
◯	Oval	Create ovals. Can also be used to create circles by pressing and holding [Shift] while dragging
🖺	Text Box	Create a box where you can insert a text memo that is not in any cell
◢	WordArt	Create a text object using the Word Art Gallery that can be resized and formatted like a graphic

Modify Graphics

Menu Method

- ☐ Select the graphic (in the following steps, *Object* refers to the object you are formatting)
- ☐ Click **Format** on the menu bar, then click *Object*, or right-click, then click **Format** *Object* on the shortcut menu
- ☐ In the Format *Object* dialog box, select the appropriate options, then click **OK**

Mouse Method

- ☐ Double-click the graphic
- ☐ In the Format *Object* dialog box, select the appropriate options, then click **OK**

Position Graphics

Mouse Method

- ☐ Select the graphic
- ☐ Move the pointer over the graphic until it changes to ✛
- ☐ Press and hold the left mouse button, then drag the object to the appropriate location

Excel Skill Set 7: Workgroup Collaboration

Convert Worksheets into Web Pages

Preview Web Pages

Menu Method

☐ Click **File** on the menu bar, then click **Web Page Preview**
☐ Click the **Close button** ☒ on the Web browser window

Create Web Pages from Worksheets

Menu Method

☐ Click **File** on the menu bar, then click **Save as Web Page**
☐ In the Save As dialog box, click the **Save in list arrow**, then navigate to the appropriate drive and folder
☐ Type the name of the file in the File name text box, then click **Save**

Create Hyperlinks

Menu Method

☐ Select the appropriate cell, range, chart, or graphic
☐ Click **Insert** on the menu bar, then click **Hyperlink** or right-click, then click **Hyperlink** on the shortcut menu
☐ In the Insert Hyperlink dialog box, select the appropriate options, then click **OK**

Button Method

☐ Select the appropriate cell, range, chart, or graphic
☐ Click the **Insert Hyperlink button** 🌐 on the Standard Buttons toolbar
☐ In the Insert Hyperlink dialog box, select the appropriate options, then click **OK**

Keyboard Method

☐ Select the appropriate cell, range, chart, or graphic
☐ Press **[Ctrl][K]**
☐ In the Insert Hyperlink dialog box, select the appropriate options, then click **OK**

Modify Hyperlinks

Menu Method

☐ Point to the **hyperlink** until the pointer becomes 🖑
☐ Right-click the **hyperlink**, then click **Edit Hyperlink** on the shortcut menu
☐ In the Edit Hyperlink dialog box, make the modifications, then click **OK**

VIEW AND EDIT COMMENTS

Attach Cell Comments

Menu Method

☐ Select the appropriate cell
☐ Click **Insert** on the menu bar, then click **Comment**, or right-click, then click **Insert Comment** on the shortcut menu
☐ Type the appropriate text in the comment balloon
☐ Click outside the comment balloon

Button Method

☐ Click the **New Comment button** on the Reviewing toolbar
☐ Follow the second and third bullets in the Attach Cell Comments Menu Method above

Edit Cell Comments

Menu Method

☐ Move the pointer over the cell marked with a comment (a red triangle in the upper-right corner of the cell)
☐ Right-click, then click **Edit Comment** on the shortcut menu
☐ Make your modifications
☐ Click outside the comment balloon

Button Method

☐ Click the cell marked with a comment (a red triangle in the upper-right corner of the cell)
☐ Click the **Edit Comment button** on the Reviewing toolbar
☐ Follow the third and fourth bullets in the Edit Cell Comments Menu Method above

Excel **EXPERT** Exam Reference

Skill Sets:

8 Importing and exporting data
9 Managing workbooks
10 Formatting numbers
11 Working with ranges
12 Customizing Excel
13 Auditing worksheets
14 Summarizing data
15 Analyzing data
16 Workgroup collaboration

Excel Skill Set 8: Importing and Exporting Data

Import Data to Excel

Import a Text File

Menu Method

- ☐ Click the upper-left cell in the range where you want Excel to import the file
- ☐ Click **Data** on the menu bar, point to **Import External Data**, then click **Import Data**
- ☐ In the Select Data Source dialog box, navigate to the appropriate drive and folder
- ☐ Click the **Files of type list arrow**, click **Text Files**, click the file, then click **Open**
- ☐ Navigate through the Text Import Wizard, making changes or accepting the defaults as appropriate to import the text file, then click **Finish**
- ☐ In the Import Data dialog box, select the appropriate option button specifying where you want the imported data to appear, then click **OK**

Import Access Database Tables

Menu Method

- ☐ Click the upper-left cell in the range where you want Excel to import the file
- ☐ Click **Data** on the menu bar, point to **Import External Data**, then click **Import Data**
- ☐ In the Select Data Source dialog box, navigate to the appropriate drive and folder
- ☐ Click the **Files of type list arrow**, click **All Data Sources** if necessary, click the **Access file**, then click **Open**

□ In the Select Table dialog box, click the table or query, then click **OK**
□ In the Import Data dialog box, select the appropriate option button specifying where you want the imported data to appear, then click **OK**

IMPORT DATA USING A QUERY

Menu Method

□ Create a blank worksheet, click **Data** on the menu bar, point to **Import External Data**, then click **New Database Query**
□ In the Choose Data Source dialog box, click **MS Access Database**, then click **OK**
□ If prompted to install the MS Access Database from the Office XP Installation CD-ROM, insert the appropriate Office XP Installation CD-ROM, and proceed through the Installation Wizard as appropriate
□ In the Select Database dialog box, navigate to the appropriate drive and folder, click the database, then click **OK**
□ Navigate through the Query Wizard, making changes or accepting the defaults as appropriate to import the database, then click **Finish**
□ In the Import Data dialog box, select the appropriate option button specifying where you want the imported data to appear, then click **OK**

IMPORT GRAPHICS

Menu Method

□ Click **Insert** on the menu bar, point to **Picture**, then click **From File**
□ In the Insert Picture dialog box, navigate to the appropriate drive and folder
□ Click the picture, then click **Insert**

Button Method

□ Click the **Insert Picture From File button** on the Drawing toolbar
□ Follow the second and third bullets in the Import Graphics Menu Method above

IMPORT DATA FROM THE WORLD WIDE WEB

Menu Method

□ Start Internet Explorer, then navigate to the Web page that contains the data to import
□ Select the data you want to import into Excel, click **Edit** on the Internet Explorer menu bar, then click **Copy**
□ Click the Microsoft Excel program button on the taskbar, then click the cell where you want to import the data
□ Click **Edit** on the Excel menu bar, then click **Paste**

Keyboard Method

□ Start Internet Explorer, then navigate to the Web page that contains the data to import
□ Select the data you want to import into Excel, then press **[Ctrl][C]**
□ Click the Microsoft Excel program button on the taskbar, then click the cell where you want to import the data
□ Press **[Ctrl][V]**

EXPORT DATA FROM EXCEL

Embed an Excel Chart in a Word Document

Menu Method

☐ In Microsoft Excel, select the chart, click **Edit** on the menu bar, then click **Copy**

☐ Start Microsoft Word, open the file or create a new document, then click where you want to embed the chart

☐ Click **Edit** on the menu bar, then click **Paste**

Button Method

☐ In Microsoft Excel, select the chart, then click the **Copy button** 🖺 on the Excel Standard Buttons toolbar

☐ Start Microsoft Word, open the file or create a new document, then click where you want to embed the chart

☐ Click the **Paste button** 🖺 on the Word Standard Buttons toolbar

Keyboard Method

☐ In Microsoft Excel, select the chart, then press **[Ctrl][C]**

☐ Start Microsoft Word, open the file or create a new document, then click where you want to embed the chart

☐ Press **[Ctrl][V]**

LINK EXCEL DATA TO A POWERPOINT PRESENTATION

Menu Method

☐ Select the cell(s) or object you want to copy

☐ Click **File** on the menu bar, then click **Copy**

☐ Start Microsoft PowerPoint, open the appropriate file or create a new presentation, then click the slide where you want to place the linked data

☐ Click **Edit** on the menu bar, then click **Paste Special**

☐ In the Paste Special dialog box, click the **Paste link option button**, then click **OK**

CONVERT A LIST TO AN ACCESS TABLE

Menu Method

☐ Start Microsoft Access, then open the appropriate file or create a new database

☐ Click **File** on the menu bar, point to **Get External Data**, then click **Import**

☐ In the Import dialog box, navigate to the appropriate drive and folder, click the **Files of type list arrow**, click **Microsoft Excel**, click the file, then click **Import**

☐ Navigate through the Import Spreadsheet Wizard, making changes or accepting the defaults as appropriate to import the spreadsheet, then click **Finish**

☐ Click **OK** in the message box

EXPORT EXCEL DATA IN XML FORMAT

Menu Method

- ☐ Click **File** on the menu bar, then click **Save As**
- ☐ In the Save As dialog box, navigate to the appropriate drive and folder
- ☐ Click the **Save as type list arrow**, click **XML Spreadsheet**, then click **Save**
- ☐ Click **Yes** in the message box if necessary

PUBLISH WORKSHEETS AND WORKBOOKS TO THE WEB

Publish a Worksheet Range to the Web

Menu Method

- ☐ Click **File** on the menu bar, then click **Save as Web Page**
- ☐ In the Save As dialog box, click **Publish**
- ☐ In the Publish as Web Page dialog box, click the **Choose list arrow**, then click **Range of cells**
- ☐ In the Publish as section, click **Browse**
- ☐ In the Publish As dialog box, navigate to the appropriate drive and folder, type the filename, then click **OK**
- ☐ In the Publish as Web Page dialog box, select any other appropriate options, then click **Publish**

PUBLISH AN INTERACTIVE WORKBOOK TO THE WEB

Menu Method

- ☐ Click **File** on the menu bar, click **Save as Web Page**
- ☐ In the Save As dialog box, click to select the **Entire Workbook option button**, click to select the **Add interactivity check box**, then click **Publish**
- ☐ In the Publish as Web Page dialog box, select any other appropriate options, then click **Publish**

USE INTERACTIVE WORKBOOKS

Menu Method

- ☐ Start Internet Explorer
- ☐ Click **File** on the menu bar, then click **Open**
- ☐ In the Open dialog box, click **Browse**
- ☐ In the Microsoft Internet Explorer dialog box, navigate to the appropriate drive and folder, click the file, then click **Open**
- ☐ In the Open dialog box, click **OK**
- ☐ Click **File** on the menu bar, click **Edit with Microsoft Excel**, make the modifications to the Excel file, then save and close in the Excel file
- ☐ To view the changes in Internet Explorer, refresh the page using Table EX-15 as a reference

Table EX-15 Internet Explorer Refresh Methods

Method	Steps
Menu	Click View on the menu bar, then click Refresh
Button	Click the Refresh button on the Internet Explorer Standard Buttons toolbar
Keyboard	Press [F5]

EXCEL SKILL SET 9: MANAGING WORKBOOKS

CREATE, EDIT, AND APPLY TEMPLATES

Create a Workbook Template

Menu Method
- ☐ Click **File** on the menu bar, then click **Save As**
- ☐ In the Save As dialog box, navigate to the appropriate drive and folder
- ☐ Click the **Save as type list arrow**, then click **Template**
- ☐ Type the filename in the File name text box, then click **Save**

CREATE A NEW WORKBOOKS BASED ON A TEMPLATE YOU CREATED

Task Pane Method
- ☐ In the New Workbook task pane, click **Choose workbook** under New from existing workbook
- ☐ In the New from Existing Workbook dialog box, navigate to the appropriate drive and folder
- ☐ Click the **Files of type list arrow**, click **All Microsoft Excel Files** if necessary, click the appropriate template, then click **Create New**
- ☐ Enter the appropriate information in the worksheet
- ☐ Click **File** on the menu bar, then click **Save As**
- ☐ In the Save As dialog box, click the **Save as type list arrow**, then click **Microsoft Excel Workbook**, if necessary
- ☐ Navigate to the appropriate drive and folder, type the filename, then click **Save**

MODIFY A WORKBOOK TEMPLATE

Menu Method
- ☐ Click **File** on the menu bar, then click **Open**
- ☐ In the Open dialog box, navigate to the appropriate drive and folder
- ☐ Click the **Files of type list arrow**, then click **Templates**
- ☐ Click the template, then click **Open**
- ☐ Make the appropriate modifications
- ☐ Click **File** on the menu bar, then click **Save**

Button Method
- ☐ Click the **Open button** 📂 on the Standard Buttons toolbar
- ☐ Follow the second through fifth bullets in the Modify a Workbook Template Menu Method above
- ☐ Click the **Save button** 💾 on the Standard Buttons toolbar

Keyboard Method
- ☐ Press **[Ctrl][O]**
- ☐ Follow the second through fifth bullets in the Modify a Workbook Template Menu Method above
- ☐ Press **[Ctrl][S]**

Task Pane Method

☐ Click **More workbooks** in the New Workbook task pane
☐ Follow the second through sixth bullets in the Modify a Workbook Template Menu Method

CREATE WORKSPACES

Create a Workspace File

Menu Method

☐ Open the appropriate files, position and resize the windows, then make any toolbar modifications to set up the workspace
☐ Click **File** on the menu bar, then click **Save Workspace**
☐ In the Save Workspace dialog box, navigate to the appropriate drive and folder, type the filename, then click **Save**
☐ If necessary, click **Yes** to save the changes to the workspace in the message box

OPEN A WORKSPACE

Menu Method

☐ Click **File** on the menu bar, then click **Open**
☐ In the Open dialog box, navigate to the appropriate drive and folder
☐ Click the **Files of type list arrow**, then click **Workspaces**
☐ Click the workspace, then click **Open**

Button Method

☐ Click the **Open button** 🖼 on the Standard Buttons toolbar
☐ Follow the second through fourth bullets in the Open a Workspace Menu Method above

Keyboard Method

☐ Press **[Ctrl][O]**
☐ Follow the second through fourth bullets in the Open a Workspace Menu Method above

Task Pane Method

☐ Click **More workbooks** in the New Workbook task pane
☐ Follow the second through fourth bullets in the Open a Workspace Menu Method above

USE DATA CONSOLIDATION

Consolidate Data from Multiple Worksheets with the Same Layout

Menu Method

☐ Select the range where the consolidated data will appear
☐ Click **Data** on the menu bar, then click **Consolidate**

☐ In the Consolidate dialog box, click the **Function list arrow**, select the appropriate function, then click the **Reference text box**
☐ Click the first worksheet, select the range, then click **Add**
☐ Click the next worksheet, verify the correct range is selected, then click **Add**
☐ Repeat for all worksheets and ranges, then click **OK**

CONSOLIDATE DATA FROM MULTIPLE WORKSHEETS WITH DIFFERENT LAYOUTS

Menu Method

☐ Click the upper-left cell in the range where the consolidated data will appear
☐ Click **Data** on the menu bar, then click **Consolidate**
☐ In the Consolidate dialog box, click the **Function list arrow**, select the appropriate function, then click the **Reference text box**
☐ Click the first worksheet, select the range, then click **Add**
☐ Repeat for all worksheets and ranges, then click **OK**

EXCEL SKILL SET 10: FORMATTING NUMBERS

CREATE AND APPLY CUSTOM NUMBER FORMATS

Create and Apply a Custom Number Format

Menu Method

☐ Click the cell or select the range to format
☐ Click **Format** on the menu bar, then click **Cells**, or right-click, then click **Format Cells** on the shortcut menu
☐ In the Format Cells dialog box, click the **Number tab**, then click **Custom** in the Category list box
☐ In the Type list box, select the format code to use as a basis, then make the modifications to this format code in the Type text box
☐ To apply additional formatting, use the Font, Alignment, and other tabs in the Format Cells dialog box, then click **OK**

Keyboard Method

☐ Click the cell or select the range to format
☐ Press **[Ctrl[1]**
☐ Follow the third through fifth bullets in the Create and Apply a Custom Number Format Menu Method above

CREATE AND APPLY A CUSTOM DATE AND TIME FORMAT

Menu Method

☐ Click the cell or select the range to format
☐ Click **Format** on the menu bar, then click **Cells**, or right-click, then click **Format Cells** on the shortcut menu
☐ In the Format Cells dialog box, click the **Number tab**, then click **Custom** in the Category list box
☐ In the Type list box, select the date and time format code to use as a basis, then make the modifications to this format code in the Type text box.
☐ To apply additional formatting, use the Font, Alignment, and other tabs in the Format Cells dialog box, then click **OK**

Keyboard Method

☐ Click the cell or select the range to format
☐ Press **[Ctrl[1]**
☐ Follow the third through fifth bullets in the Create and Apply a Custom Date and Time Format Menu Method above

CREATE AND APPLY A CUSTOM FORMAT WITH TEXT

Menu Method

☐ Click the cell or select the range to format
☐ Click **Format** on the menu bar, then click **Cells**, or right-click, then click **Format Cells** on the shortcut menu

☐ In the Format Cells dialog box, click the **Number tab**, then click **Custom** in the Category list box
☐ In the Type list box, select the format code to use as a basis, click in the Type text box after the last character, then type the text to appear surrounded by quotation marks
☐ To apply additional formatting, use the Font, Alignment, and other tabs in the Format Cells dialog box, then click **OK**

Keyboard Method

☐ Click the cell or select the range to format
☐ Press **[Ctrl][1]**
☐ Follow the third through fifth bullets in the Create and Apply a Custom Format with Text Menu Method above

USE CONDITIONAL FORMATS

Menu Method

☐ Click the cell or select the range to format
☐ Click **Format** on the menu bar, then click **Conditional Formatting**
☐ In the Conditional Formatting dialog box, select the appropriate conditions for the first condition, then click **Format**
☐ In the Format Cells dialog box, click the appropriate options, then click **OK**
☐ In the Conditional Formatting dialog box, click **Add**, repeat the third and fourth bullets for additional conditional formatting as appropriate, then click **OK**

Excel Skill Set 11: Working with Ranges

Use Named Ranges in Formulas

Create a Cell or Range Name

Menu Method

- ☐ Select the range
- ☐ Click the **Name box** to the far left of the Formula bar, type the range name, then press **[Enter]**

OR

- ☐ Select the range
- ☐ Click **Insert** on the menu bar, point to **Name**, then click **Define**
- ☐ In the Define Name dialog box, type the range name in the Name in workbook textbox, then click **OK**

Use Labels to Create Range Names

Menu Method

- ☐ Select the range, including any row or column labels
- ☐ Click **Insert** on the menu bar, point to **Name**, then click **Create**
- ☐ In the Create Names dialog box, click the appropriate check box to use as the range name, then click **OK**

Use a Named Range Reference in One or More Formulas

Keyboard Method

- ☐ Click the cell where the formula will appear
- ☐ Type the formula in the cell or in the Formula bar, inserting the range name whose values are to be used in the formula where appropriate, then press **[Enter]** or **[Tab]**

Use Lookup and Reference Functions

Use VLOOKUP or HLOOKUP to Find Values in a List

Menu Method

- ☐ Click the cell where the formula will appear
- ☐ Click **Insert** on the menu bar, then click **Function**
- ☐ In the Insert Function dialog box, click the **Or select a category list arrow**, then click **All**
- ☐ Double-click **VLOOKUP** or **HLOOKUP** from the Select a function list box
- ☐ In the Function Arguments dialog box, select the appropriate options using Table EX-16 as a reference, then click **OK**

Menu Method

☐ Click the cell where the formula is to appear
☐ Click the **Insert Function button** f_x on the Formula bar
☐ Follow the third through fifth bullets in the Using VLOOKUP or
   HLOOKUP to Find Values in a List Menu Method above

Table EX-16 VLOOKUP and HLOOKUP Function Arguments

Argument	Definition
lookup_value	The value in the first column of the array; can be a value, a reference, or a text string
table_array	The table of information in which data is looked up; use a reference to a range or range name. There are sorting requirements depending on the range_lookup value.
col_index_num (VLOOKUP) OR row_index_num (HLOOKUP)	The column or row number in table_array from which the matching value must be returned
range_lookup (optional)	A logical value that specifies whether you want VLOOKUP to find an exact match or an approximate match. If range_lookup is TRUE, or there is no value in the formula, the match is approximate. If FALSE is entered as the range_lookup, the match returned will be exact, or there will be an error if there is no exact value.

EXCEL SKILL SET 12: CUSTOMIZING EXCEL

CUSTOMIZE TOOLBARS AND MENUS

Add a Custom Menu

Menu Method

- ☐ Click **Tools** on the menu bar, then click **Customize**, or rght-click any toolbar, then click **Customize** on the shortcut menu
- ☐ In the Customize dialog box, click the **Commands tab**, then click **New Menu** in the Categories list box
- ☐ In the Commands list box, click **New Menu**, press and hold the left mouse button, drag the menu until the **position indicator** ⌶ and the **menu position pointer** 🖳 are over the menu bar to the right of the Help menu, then release the mouse button
- ☐ With the Customize dialog box still open, right-click **New Menu** on the menu bar, point to **Name**, drag to select **New menu**, type the menu name, then press **[Enter]**
- ☐ Click the appropriate option in the Categories list, drag each **command** from the Commands list box over the **menu** and down under the menu name to place the command on the menu, then release the mouse button
- ☐ Click **Close** in the Customize dialog box

ADD TOOLBAR BUTTONS

Button Method

- ☐ Click the **Toolbar Options button** 🖼 on the right side of the toolbar you want to customize
- ☐ Point to **Add or Remove Buttons**, then point to the toolbar name
- ☐ In the toolbar button list, click the checkbox for the button you want to add, then click anywhere in the worksheet

REMOVE TOOLBARS BUTTONS

Menu Method

- ☐ Click the **Toolbar Options button** 🖼 on the right side of the toolbar you want to customize
- ☐ Point to **Add or Remove Buttons**, then point to the toolbar name
- ☐ In the toolbar button list, click the check box for button you want to delete, then click anywhere in the worksheet

Keyboard Method

- ☐ Press and hold **[Alt]**, then position the ⌖ pointer over the button to delete
- ☐ Drag the button from the toolbar to the worksheet area to remove it

CREATE, EDIT, AND RUN MACROS

Record a Macro

Menu Method

- ☐ Click **Tools** on the menu bar, point to **Macro**, then click **Record New Macro**
- ☐ In the Record Macro dialog box, type the macro name in the Macro name text box
- ☐ Click the **Store macro in list arrow**, then click the appropriate macro storage option
- ☐ To assign a keyboard shortcut to the macro, click the **Shortcut key text box**, then type the key
- ☐ Click **OK**
- ☐ Perform the actions for the macro
- ☐ Click **Tools** on the menu bar, point to **Macro**, then click **Stop Recording**

RUN A MACRO

Menu Method

- ☐ Click **Tools** on the menu bar, point to **Macro**, then click **Macros**
- ☐ In the Macro dialog box, click the appropriate macro, then click **Run**

Keyboard Method

- ☐ Press **[Alt][F8]**
- ☐ In the Macro dialog box, click the appropriate macro, then click **Run**

OR

- ☐ Press the keyboard combination you assigned to the macro if appropriate

EDIT A MACRO

Menu Method

- ☐ Click **Tools** on the menu bar, point to **Macro**, then click **Macros**
- ☐ In the Macro dialog box, select the appropriate macro, then click **Edit**
- ☐ In the Microsoft Visual Basic window, make the modifications to the macro code
- ☐ Click File on the menu bar, then click **Close and Return to Microsoft Excel**

Keyboard Method

- ☐ Press **[Alt][F8]**
- ☐ In the Macro dialog box, select the appropriate macro, then click **Edit**
- ☐ In the Microsoft Visual Basic window, make the modifications to the macro code
- ☐ Press **[Alt][Q]**

EXCEL SKILL SET 13: AUDITING WORKSHEETS

AUDIT FORMULAS

Trace Precedents

Menu Method

☐ Click the cell that contains the formula
☐ Click **Tools** on the menu bar, point to **Formula Auditing**, then click **Trace Precedents**
☐ Double-click the **blue arrow** to navigate between the cells

Button Method

☐ Click the cell that contains the formula
☐ Click the **Trace Precedents button** 📲 on the Formula Auditing toolbar
☐ Double-click the **blue arrow** to navigate between the cells

TRACE DEPENDENTS

Menu Method

☐ Click the cell that that is referenced in a formula
☐ Click **Tools** on the menu bar, point to **Formula Auditing**, then click **Trace Dependents**
☐ Double-click the **blue arrow** to navigate between the cells

Button Method

☐ Click the cell that is referenced in a formula
☐ Click the **Trace Dependents button** 📄 on the Formula Auditing toolbar
☐ Double-click the **blue arrow** to navigate between the cells

LOCATE AND RESOLVE ERRORS

Menu Method

☐ Click the cell that shows an error, using Table EX-17 as a reference
☐ Click **Tools** on the menu bar, point to **Formula Auditing**, then click **Trace Error**
☐ Use the Formula bar to correct the formula

Button Method

☐ Click the cell that shows an error, using Table EX-17 as a reference
☐ Click the **Trace Error button** 🔷 on the Formula Auditing toolbar to display precedents and dependents in the formula
☐ Use the Formula bar to correct the formula

Table EX-17　Common Cell Errors

Error	Means
#DIV/0!	Value is divided by zero
#NAME?	Excel does not recognize text
#N/A	Value is not available for the formula
#NULL!	When a formula specifies an intersection of two areas that do not intersect
#NUM	Invalid formula number(s)
#REF	Invalid cell reference
#VALUE	Operand or argument is incorrect

IDENTIFY DEPENDENCIES IN FORMULAS

Menu Method

☐ Click the cell that contains the formula
☐ Click **Tools** on the menu bar, point to **Formula Auditing**, then click **Evaluate Formula**
☐ In the Evaluate Formula dialog box, click the appropriate button, using Table EX-18 as a reference

Button Method

☐ Click the cell that contains the formula
☐ Click the **Evaluate Formula button** 🔍 on the Formula Auditing toolbar
☐ In the Evaluate Formula dialog box, click the appropriate button, using Table EX-18 as a reference

Table EX-18　Evaluate Formula Dialog Box Options

Button	Used to
Evaluate	Shows the result of the underlined value; click repeatedly to display additional levels of the formula
Step In	View the formula that supports the highlighted argument; available when there is a formula within the formula you are evaluating
Step Out	Display the value in the cell; available after you have clicked Step In
Restart	Return to the highest level of the formula, then restart the evaluation process

REMOVE ALL TRACER ARROWS

Menu Method

☐ Click **Tools** on the menu bar, point to **Formula Auditing**, then click **Remove All Arrows**

Button Method

☐ Click the **Remove All Arrows button** 🔍 on the Formula Auditing toolbar

Excel Skill Set 14: Summarizing Data

Use Subtotals with Lists and Ranges

Sort a List by One Field

Menu Method

- ☐ Make sure the data you want to sort is in list format, that each column has a label in the first row and contains similar data, and that there are no blank rows or columns
- ☐ Click a cell in the column to sort
- ☐ Click **Data** on the menu bar, then click **Sort**
- ☐ In the Sort dialog box, click the **Sort by list arrow**, then click the **row header**
- ☐ Click the **Ascending** or **Descending option button** as appropriate, then click **OK**

Sort a List by Two Fields

Menu Method

- ☐ Click any cell in the range which you want to sort
- ☐ Click **Data** on the menu bar, then click **Sort**
- ☐ In the Sort dialog box, click the **Sort by list arrow**, then click the **row header**
- ☐ Click the **Ascending** or **Descending option button** as appropriate
- ☐ Click the first **Then by list arrow**, then click the **row header**
- ☐ Click the **Ascending** or **Descending option button** as appropriate, then click **OK**

Subtotal a List

Menu Method

- ☐ Sort the list as appropriate so that the rows to subtotal are together
- ☐ Click any cell in the range which you want to subtotal
- ☐ Click **Data** on the menu bar, then click **Subtotals**
- ☐ In the Subtotal dialog box, click the **At each change in list arrow**, then click the **row** or **column header** if necessary
- ☐ Click the **Use function list arrow**, then click the appropriate check box
- ☐ In the Add subtotal to list box, click the appropriate option
- ☐ Make any other appropriate selections, then click **OK**

Define and Apply Filters

Create a Custom Filter

Menu Method

- ☐ Click **Data** on the menu bar, point to **Filter**, then click **AutoFilter**
- ☐ Click the **AutoFilter list arrow** for the row you want to customize, then click **(Custom)**
- ☐ In the Custom AutoFilter dialog box, select the appropriate filter options, then click **OK**

CREATE AN ADVANCED FILTER

Menu Method

☐ Insert at least three blank rows above the list that can be used as a criteria range

☐ In the first blank row, copy the column labels from the list

☐ In the second blank row, enter the filter criteria, using Table EX-19 as a reference, then leave at least one blank row above the list

☐ Click anywhere in the list range, click **Data** on the menu bar, point to **Filter**, then click **Advanced Filter**

☐ In the Advanced Filter dialog box, to filter the list by hiding rows that don't match your criteria, click the **Filter the list, in-place option button**

☐ To filter the list by copying rows that match your criteria to another area of the worksheet, click the **Copy to another location option button**, click the **Copy to text box**, then click the upper-left cell of the area where you want to paste the rows

☐ In the **List range text box**, verify that the range reference is correct

☐ Click the **Criteria range text box**, click the worksheet, then select the rows containing the criteria labels and filter criteria (Note: this will be the first and second of the three rows you inserted)

☐ Click **OK**

Table EX-19 Filter Criteria Operands

Use	To find
Text	All items that begin with that text. For instance, *Ma* finds "Mary" and "Margaret"
=""=text"	To find only the specified text
? (question mark)	Any single character. For example, jo?s finds "jons" and "joes"
* (asterisk)	Any number of characters. For example, *ary finds "Canary" and "Sanctuary"
~ (tilde) followed by ?, *, or ~	A question mark, asterisk, or tilde. For example, Guest~? finds "Guest?", and Taxi~* finds "Taxi*"
<*number*	All numbers less than that number. For example, <7 finds all numbers less than 7
<=*number*	All numbers less than or equal to that number. For example, <10 finds all numbers less than 10, and also all instances of 10
>*number*	All numbers greater than that number. For example, <15 finds all numbers greater than 15
>=*number*	All numbers greater than or equal to that number. For example, <100 finds all numbers greater than 100, and also all instances of 100
<> *number*	All numbers, except for that number

ADD GROUP AND OUTLINE CRITERIA TO RANGES

Menu Method

☐ Sort the range if necessary, then click anywhere in the range
☐ Click **Data** on the menu bar, point to **Group and Outline**, then click **Auto Outline**
☐ Use Table EX-20 as a reference to display and hide the outline levels and details

Table EX-20 Outline Buttons

Button	Use
–	Hide the details
+	Show the details
1 , 2	Show the row or column levels

USE DATA VALIDATION

Validate Entered Data

Menu Method

☐ Select the range
☐ Click **Data** on the menu bar, then click **Validation**
☐ In the Data Validation dialog box, click the appropriate options using Table EX-21 as a reference, then click **OK**

Table EX-21 Data Validation Dialog Box Tabs

Tab	Use to
Settings	Set validation criteria for input data
Input Message	Set a message which will appear when a user selects a cell in the range
Error Alert	Set a message which will appear when a user enters data that does not meet validation criteria

RETRIEVE EXTERNAL DATA AND CREATE QUERIES

Use XML to Share Excel Data on the Web

Menu Method

☐ Click **File** on the menu bar, then click **Save As**
☐ In the Save As dialog box, navigate to the appropriate drive and folder
☐ Click the Save as type list arrow, click **XML Spreadsheet**, then click **Save**
☐ Click **Yes** in the message box if necessary

☐ Start **Internet Explorer**, click **File** on the menu bar, then click **Open**

☐ In the Open dialog box, click **Browse**, then in the Microsoft Internet Explorer dialog box, navigate to the appropriate drive and folder

☐ Click the **Files of type list arrow**, click **All Files**, click the **XML file**, then click **Open**

☐ In the Open dialog box, click **OK**

CREATE EXTENSIBLE MARKUP LANGUAGE (XML) WEB QUERIES

Create XML Web Queries

Menu Method

☐ Connect to the Internet and open a blank worksheet

☐ Click **Data** on the menu bar, point to **Import External Data**, then click **New Web Query**

☐ In the New Web Query dialog box, click the **Address text box**, type the path to the appropriate drive and folder followed by the XML file-name, then click **Go**

☐ Click the ▶ for each table you want to import, so that it changes to ☑, then click **Import**

☐ In the Import Data dialog box, select the appropriate options, then click **OK**

EXCEL SKILL SET 15: ANALYZING DATA

CREATE PIVOTTABLE REPORTS AND PIVOTCHART REPORTS

Create a PivotTable Report

Menu Method

- ☐ Click anywhere within the list range
- ☐ Click **Data** on the menu bar, then click **PivotTable and PivotChart Report**
- ☐ Navigate through the PivotTable and PivotChart Wizard, making changes or accepting the defaults as appropriate to create the PivotTable, then click **Finish**
- ☐ Drag each field from the PivotTable Field list to the appropriate area on the PivotTable, or click the field in the PivotTable Field list, click the **Add To list arrow**, select the area, then click **Add To**

MODIFY A PIVOTTABLE REPORT

Use Table EX-22 and Table EX-23 to make changes to a PivotTable Report.

Table EX-22

Modification type	Steps
Add an item field	☐ Click the Show Field List button 🔲 on the PivotTable toolbar if necessary
	☐ Drag each field from the PivotTable Field list to the appropriate area on the PivotTable, or click the field in the PivotTable Field list, click the Add To list arrow, select the area, then click Add To
Rename an item	☐ Click the item, type the new name, then press [Enter]
Formatting	☐ See the activity "Format a PivotTable Report"

Table EX-23 Selected PivotTable Toolbar Buttons

Button	Menu	Use to
Format Report	Click Format on the menu bar, then click Cells or AutoFormat, or right-click, then click Format Cells	Open the AutoFormat or Format Cells dialog box to apply table and report formats
Chart Wizard	Click Insert on the menu bar, then click Chart, or right-click the PivotTable, then click PivotChart	Create a PivotChart report from your PivotTable
Field Settings		Change summary function of selected fields
Show Field List or Hide Field List	Right-click the PivotTable, then click Show Field List or Hide Field List	Display or close the Field List window

UPDATE A PIVOTTABLE REPORT

Menu Method

☐ Modify the report as appropriate
☐ Click **Data** on the menu bar, then click **Refresh Data**, or right-click the PivotTable, then click **Refresh Data**

Button Method

☐ Modify the report as appropriate
☐ Click the **Refresh Data button** 🔽 on the PivotTable toolbar

FORMAT A PIVOTTABLE REPORT

Menu Method

☐ Select the cells to format
☐ Click **Format** on the menu bar, then click **Cells**, or right-click, then click **Format Cells** on the shortcut menu
☐ In the Format Cells dialog box, select the appropriate options, then click **OK**

Button Method

☐ Click any cell inside the PivotTable
☐ Click the **Format Report button** 📋 on the PivotTable toolbar
☐ In the AutoFormat dialog box, select the the appropriate format, then click **OK**

Keyboard Method

☐ Click the cell or select the range to format
☐ Press **[Ctrl][1]**
☐ In the Format Cells dialog box, select the appropriate options, then click **OK**

CREATE A PIVOTCHART REPORT

Menu Method

☐ Click anywhere within the list range

☐ Click **Data** on the menu bar, then click **PivotTable and PivotChart Report**

☐ In the first PivotTable and PivotChart Wizard dialog box, click the **PivotChart report (with PivotTable report) option button**

☐ Navigate through the rest of the PivotTable and PivotChart Wizard, making changes or accepting the defaults as appropriate to create the PivotChart Report, then click **Finish**

☐ Drag each field from the PivotTable Field list to the appropriate area, or click the field in the PivotTable Field list, click the **Add To list arrow**, select the area, then click **Add To**

MODIFY A PIVOTCHART REPORT

Menu Method

☐ Click the appropriate chart object to select it (in the following steps, *object* refers to the object you are formatting)

☐ Click **Format** on the menu bar, then click **Selected *Object***, or right-click the object, then click **Format *Object***

☐ In the Format *Object* dialog box, select the appropriate options, then click **OK**

Button Method

☐ Click the appropriate chart object to select it (in the following steps, *object* refers to the object you are formatting)

☐ Click the **Format *Object* button** 🖼 on the Chart toolbar

☐ In the Format *Object* dialog box, select the appropriate options, then click **OK**

Mouse Method

☐ Double-click the appropriate chart object to select it

☐ In the Format *Object* dialog box, select the appropriate options, then click **OK**

FORECAST VALUES WITH WHAT-IF ANALYSIS

Create a Trendline

Menu Method

☐ Click any column on the chart for the series for which you want to create a trendline

☐ Click **Chart** on the menu bar, then click **Add Trendline**

☐ In the Add Trendline dialog box, click the appropriate options, then click **OK**

CREATE AND DISPLAY SCENARIOS

Menu Method

- ☐ Click the appropriate cell
- ☐ Click **Tools** on the menu bar, then click **Scenarios**
- ☐ In the Scenario Manager dialog box, click **Add**
- ☐ In the Add Scenario dialog box, click the **Scenario name box**, then type the scenario name
- ☐ Click the **Changing cells text box**, select the cell or range, click other appropriate options, then click **OK**
- ☐ In the Scenario Values dialog box, enter a value for the cells to change
- ☐ If necessary, click **Add**, then repeat the fourth through sixth bullets to add another scenario
- ☐ Click **OK**
- ☐ In the Scenario Manager dialog box, click the appropriate scenario, click **Show**, then click **Close**

EXCEL SKILL SET 16: WORKGROUP COLLABORATION

MODIFY PASSWORDS, PROTECTIONS, AND PROPERTIES

Protect Worksheet Cells

Menu Method

☐ Select the range
☐ Click **Format** on the menu bar, then click **Cells**, or right-click, then click **Format Cells** on the shortcut menu
☐ In the Format Cells dialog box, click the **Protection tab**, make sure the **Locked check box** is checked, then click **OK**
☐ Click **Tools** on the menu bar, point to **Protection**, then click **Protect Sheet**
☐ In the Protect Sheet dialog box, click to select the **Protect worksheet and contents of locked cells check box** if necessary
☐ Click **OK**
☐ In the Confirm Password dialog box, retype the password, then click **OK**

PROTECT WORKSHEETS

Menu Method

☐ Click **Tools** on the menu bar, point to **Protection**, then click **Protect Sheet**
☐ In the Protect Sheet dialog box, click the **Protect worksheet and contents of locked cells check box** to select it, if necessary
☐ In the Password to unprotect sheet text box, type the password if necessary
☐ Click the appropriate features a user can access, then click **OK**
☐ If necessary, in the Confirm Password dialog box, type the password, then click **OK**

PROTECT WORKBOOKS

Menu Method

☐ Click **File** on the menu bar, click **Save As**
☐ In the Save As dialog box, click **Tools** on the toolbar, then click **General Options**
☐ In the Save Options dialog box, click the **Password to open text box**, then type the password
☐ Click the **Password to modify text box**, type a different password, then click **OK**
☐ For each password dialog box, confirm the password by typing it in the password text box, then clicking **OK**
☐ In the Save As dialog box, click **Save**

PROTECT WORKBOOK ELEMENTS

Menu Method

☐ Click **Tools** on the menu bar, point to **Protection**, then click **Protect Workbook**
☐ In the Protect Workbook dialog box, select the appropriate checkboxes
☐ If necessary, click the password text box, type the password, then click **OK**
☐ If necessary, type the password to confirm it, then click **OK**

CREATE A SHARED WORKBOOK

Menu Method

☐ Click **Tools** on the menu bar, then click **Share Workbook**
☐ In the Share Workbook dialog box, click the **Editing tab** if necessary, click the **Allow changes by more than one user at the same time check box** if necessary, then click **OK**
☐ Click **OK** if prompted to save the file
☐ In the Save As dialog box, type the filename in the Filename text box, then click **Save**

TRACK, ACCEPT, AND REJECT CHANGES TO WORKBOOKS

Track Worksheet Changes

Menu Method

☐ Click **Tools** on the menu bar, point to **Track Changes**, then click **Highlight Changes**
☐ In the Highlight Changes dialog box, click to select the **Track changes while editing check box**
☐ Click to select the **Highlight changes on screen check box** if necessary, then click **OK**
☐ In the message box, click **OK** if necessary

ACCEPT AND REJECT CHANGES

Menu Method

☐ Click **Tools** on the menu bar, point to **Track Changes**, then click **Accept or Reject Changes**
☐ If you get a message box to save the workbook, click **OK**
☐ In the Select Changes to Accept or Reject dialog box, in the When list box, make sure **Not yet reviewed** is selected, then click **OK**
☐ In the Accept or Reject Changes dialog box, click the appropriate options

REVIEW CHANGES

Menu Method

☐ Click **Tools** on the menu bar, point to **Track Changes**, then click **Highlight Changes**

☐ In the Highlight Changes dialog box, click the **Track changes while editing check box** to select this option

☐ Click to select the **Highlight changes on screen check box** if necessary, then click **OK**

☐ Position the insertion point over a cell with a colored triangle in the corner, then read the screen tip to review the change

MERGE WORKBOOKS

Menu Method

☐ Open the original shared workbook

☐ Click **Tools** on the menu bar, then click **Compare and Merge Workbooks**

☐ Click **OK** if prompted to save the file

☐ In the Select File to Merge Into Current Workbook dialog box, click the file, then click **OK**

☐ Click **Tools** on the menu bar, point to **Track Changes**, then click **Highlight Changes**

☐ Click the **When list arrow**, then click **All**

☐ Click to select the **List changes on a new sheet check box**, then click **OK**

MICROSOFT ACCESS 2002
EXAM REFERENCE

Getting Started with Access 2002

The Access MOUS exams assume a basic level of proficiency in Access. This section is intended to help you reference these basic skills while you are preparing to take the Access Core or Expert exams.

> ☐ Starting and exiting Access
> ☐ Viewing the database window
> ☐ Using toolbars
> ☐ Using task panes
> ☐ Opening and closing databases
> ☐ Navigating in the database window
> ☐ Saving databases
> ☐ Getting Help

START AND EXIT ACCESS

Start Access

Button Method

☐ Click the Start button **🏁Start** on the Windows taskbar
☐ Point to Programs or **All Programs**
☐ Click Microsoft Access

   OR

☐ Double-click the Microsoft Access program icon 🗔 on the desktop

Exit Access

Menu Method

☐ Click **File** on the menu bar, then click **Exit**

Button Method

☐ Click the **Close button** ☒ on the program window title bar

VIEW THE DATABASE WINDOW

Figure AC-1   The Access Window

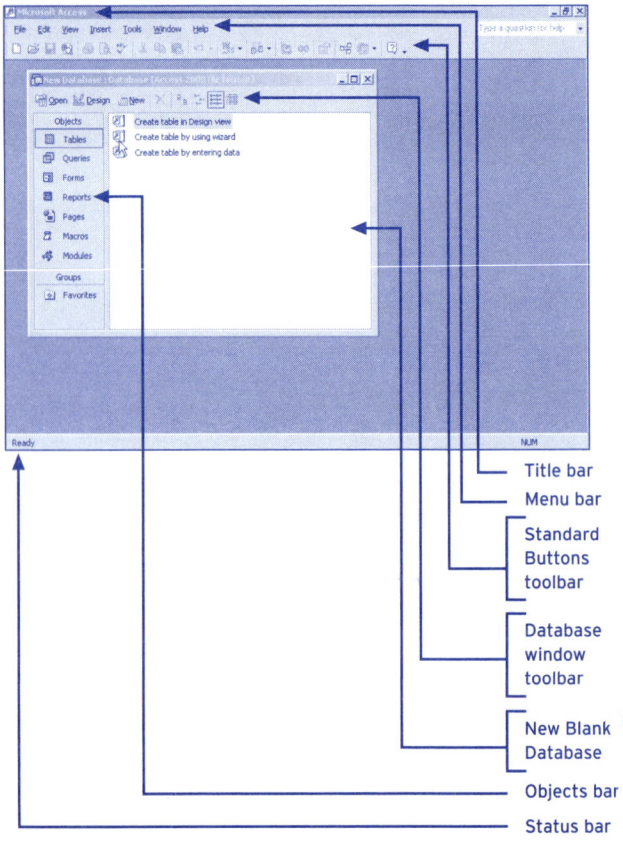

Title bar

Menu bar

Standard Buttons toolbar

Database window toolbar

New Blank Database

Objects bar

Status bar

USE TOOLBARS

Display Toolbars

Menu Method

☐ Click **View** on the menu bar, point to **Toolbars**, then click the toolbar to display

OR

☐ Right-click any toolbar, then click the toolbar to display on the shortcut menu

Customize Toolbars

Menu Method

☐ Click **Tools** on the menu bar, then click **Customize**, or click **view** on the menu bar, point to **Toolbars**, then click **Customize**, or right-click any toolbar, then click **Customize** on the shortcut menu

☐ In the Customize dialog box, select the appropriate options, then click **Close**

Button Method

☐ Click the **Toolbar Options button** ⌄ on the toolbar to customize

☐ Point to Add or Remove Buttons, then click Customize

☐ Follow the steps in the second and third bullets in the Customize Toolbars Menu Method above

Reposition Toolbars

Mouse Method

☐ To move a toolbar, position the pointer over the left edge of the toolbar (not over a button)

☐ When the pointer changes to ↔, press and hold the mouse button

☐ Drag the toolbar to a blank area of the window or to a different location, then release the mouse button

USE TASK PANES

Menu Method

☐ If the task pane is not open, click **View** on the menu bar, point to **Toolbars**, then click **Task Pane** or right-click the toolbar, then click **Task Pane** on the shortcut menu

☐ Click the **Other Task Panes list arrow** ▼ on the task pane title bar, then click the appropriate task pane to switch to another pane

☐ Click the **Back button** ⬦ on the task pane title bar to return to the previously displayed task pane

☐ Click the **Close button** ✕ on the task pane title bar to close the task pane

OPEN AND CLOSE DATABASES

Open an Existing Database

Menu Method

☐ Click **File** on the menu bar, then click **Open**

☐ In the Open dialog box, navigate to the appropriate drive and folder

☐ Click the file, then click **Open**

Button Method

☐ Click the **Open button** 🗁 on the Standard Buttons toolbar

☐ Follow the second and third bullets in the Open an Existing Database Menu Method above

Keyboard Method

☐ Press [Ctrl][O]

☐ Follow the second and third bullets in the Open an Existing Database Menu Method above

Task Pane Method

☐ Click a database under the Open a file section of the New File task pane
or click **More files** under the Open a file section, then follow the second
and third bullets in the Open an Existing Database Menu Method above
to open an existing database

Close Databases

Menu Method

☐ Close all database objects, and make the database window active
☐ Click **File** on the menu bar, then click **Close**
☐ If prompted to save the database or an object, click Yes or No as appropriate

Button Method

☐ Close all database objects, and make the database window active
☐ Click the **Close Window button** ☒ on the menu bar if the database window is maximized, or on the database window title bar if the database
window is not maximized
☐ If prompted to save the database or an object, click Yes or No as
appropriate

Keyboard Method

☐ Close all database objects, and make the database window active
☐ Press **[Ctrl][W]**
☐ If prompted to save the database or an object, click Yes or No as
appropriate

SAVE DATABASES

Menu Method

☐ Open the object
☐ Click **File** on the menu bar, then click **Save**

Button Method

☐ Open the object
☐ Click the **Save button** 🖫 on the Standard Buttons toolbar

Keyboard Method

☐ Open the object
☐ Press **[Ctrl][S]**

GET HELP

Menu Method

☐ Click **Help** on the menu bar, then click **Microsoft Access Help**
☐ Use Table AC-1 as a reference to select the most appropriate way to
search for help using the Microsoft Access Help window

Button Method

☐ Click the **Microsoft Access Help button** ⍰ on the Standard Buttons
toolbar

☐ Use Table AC-1 as a reference to select the most appropriate way to search for help using the Microsoft Access Help window

OR

☐ Click the **Ask a Question box** Type a question for help ▾ on the menu bar
☐ Type your question, then press **[Enter]**
☐ Select the option you want from the drop down list, then read about your question in the Microsoft Access Help window, using Table AC-1 as a reference

Keyboard Method

☐ Press **[F1]**
☐ Use Table AC-1 as a reference to select the most appropriate way to search for help using the Microsoft Access Help window

Table AC-1 Microsoft Help Window Tabs

Tab	To use:
Contents	Click the **Expand indicator** ＋ next to each topic you want to explore further, then click the selection you want and read the results in the right pane
Answer Wizard	Type your question in the What would you like to do? text box, click **Search**, then read the results in the right pane
Index	Type the keyword(s) you want to search for in the Type keywords text box, click **Search**, then read the results in the right pane

Access CORE Exam Reference

Skill Sets:

1 Creating and using databases
2 Creating and modifying tables
3 Creating and modifying queries
4 Creating and modifying forms
5 Viewing and organizing information
6 Defining relationships
7 Producing reports
8 Integrating with other applications

Access Skill Set 1: Creating and Using Databases

Create Access Databases

Menu Method
- ☐ Click **File** on the menu bar, then click **New**
- ☐ In the New File task pane, click **General Templates** in the New from template section
- ☐ In the Templates dialog box, click the appropriate tab, click the appropriate template, then click **OK**
- ☐ In the File New Database dialog box, navigate to the appropriate drive and folder, type the filename, then click **Create**
- ☐ If necessary, navigate through the Database Wizard, making changes or accepting the defaults as appropriate to create the database, then click **Finish**

Button Method
- ☐ Click the **New button** 🗋 on the Standard Buttons toolbar
- ☐ Follow the steps in the second through fifth bullets of the Create Access Databases Menu Method above

Keyboard Method
- ☐ Press **[Ctrl][N]**
- ☐ Follow the steps in the second through fifth bullets of the Create Access Databases Menu Method above

Open Database Objects in Multiple Views

Menu Method
- ☐ On the Objects bar, click the button for the object type to view
- ☐ Right-click the object to view
- ☐ On the shortcut menu, click **Open** to edit the object, or **Design View** to modify the object's design, using Table AC-2 as a reference

Button Method
- ☐ On the Objects bar, click the button for the object type to view
- ☐ Click the **Open button** 📝 on the Database window toolbar to open the object in a view used for editing data, or the **Design button** 🔧 on

the Database window toolbar to open the object in Design View, using Table AC-2 as a reference

Keyboard Method
□ On the Objects bar, click the button for the object type to view
□ Click the object to view, then press **[Enter]** to open it in the view used to edit data

Mouse Method
□ Click the button for the object type to view on the Objects bar
□ Double-click the object to view to open it in the view used to edit data

Table AC-2 Database Views

Object	View	Used to
Form	Form View	Edit and enter data
	Form Design View	Modify the design and structure of the form
Report	Print Preview	View a report on the screen before you print it
	Report Design View	Change the layout and format of the report
Table	Table Design View	Add or delete fields
	Table Datasheet View	Find, edit, and enter records
Query	Query Design View	Modify the query
	Query Datasheet View	Find, edit, and enter records

MOVE AMONG RECORDS

Open the object to navigate through, then use the techniques in Table AC-3 and Table AC-10 to move to the desired location in the object.

Table AC-3 Common Navigation Techniques

Keyboard key or key combination	Moves to the following location
⬆	Same field in the previous record
⬇	Same field in the next record
➡, [Enter] or [Tab]	Next field
⬅, or [Shift][Tab]	Previous field
⬆ or [Shift][Tab]	Previous field (Form View)
⬇ or [Tab]	Next field (Form View)
[Ctrl][Home]	First field of the first record
[Home]	First field of the current record
[Ctrl][End]	Last field of the last record
[End]	Last field of the current record
[Page Down] or [Page Up]	Down or up one screen at a time

Navigate Through Subdatasheets

Menu Method

☐ Open the table in Datasheet View
☐ Click **Format** on the menu bar, point to **Subdatasheet**, then click **Expand All** to access all subdatasheets or click **Collapse All** to hide all subdatasheets

Button Method

☐ Open the table in Datasheet View
☐ Click the Expand button **+** next to the record to open its subdatasheet, or click the **Collapse button** **−** to hide the record's subdatasheet

FORMAT DATASHEETS

Menu Method

☐ Open the table or query
☐ Click **Format** on the menu bar, click **Font**, then select the appropriate options in the Font dialog box using Figure AC-2 as a reference

Button Method

☐ Open the table or query
☐ Select the appropriate format options from the buttons on the Formatting toolbar using Table AC-4 as a reference

Keyboard Method

☐ Open the table or query
☐ Press the appropriate keyboard combination using Table AC-4 as a reference

Figure AC-2   Font dialog box

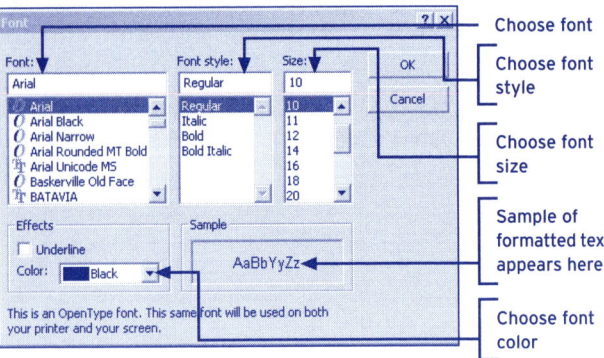

Table AC-4 Button and Keyboard Methods for Applying Formatting Effects

Formatting Effect	Used to	Formatting toolbar button	Keyboard
Font	Select a font type	Arial	
Font Size	Select a font size	10	
Bold	Turn bold font style on and off	**B**	[Ctrl][B]
Italic	Turn italic font style on and off	*I*	[Ctrl][I]
Underline	Turn underline font style on and off	U	[Ctrl][U]
Fill/Back Color	Change the datasheet background color		
Font/Fore Color	Change the datasheet text color		
Line/Border Color	Change the datasheet gridline color		
Gridlines	Determine which gridlines appear on the datasheet		
Special Effect	Change the effect (flat, raised, or sunken) of the datasheet cells		

ACCESS SKILL SET 2: CREATING AND MODIFYING TABLES

CREATE AND MODIFY TABLES

Create Tables Using the Table Wizard

Menu Method

- ☐ Click **Insert** on the menu bar, click **Table**, click **Table Wizard** in the New Table dialog box, then click **OK**
- ☐ Navigate through the Table Wizard, making changes or accepting the defaults as appropriate to create the table, then click **Finish**

    OR

- ☐ Click the **Tables button** [Tables] on the Objects bar, right-click **Create table by using wizard**, then click **Open** on the shortcut menu
- ☐ Navigate through the Table Wizard, making changes or accepting the defaults as appropriate to create the table, then click **Finish**

Button Method

- ☐ Click the **Tables button** [Tables] on the Objects bar
- ☐ Click the **New button** [ ] on the Database window toolbar
- ☐ In the New Table dialog box, click **Table Wizard**, then click **OK**
- ☐ Follow the steps in the second bullet of the Create Tables Using the Table Wizard Menu Method above

    OR

- ☐ Click the **Tables button** [Tables] on the Objects bar, then double-click **Create table by using wizard**
- ☐ Follow the steps in the second bullet of the Create Tables Using the Table Wizard Menu Method above

Create Tables Using Table Design View

Menu Method

- ☐ Click **Insert** on the menu bar, then click **Table**
- ☐ In the New Table dialog box, click **Design View**, then click **OK**
- ☐ For each field, type the field name in the Field Name column, then press **[Enter]**
- ☐ To specify the type of data, click the **Data Type list arrow**, then click the appropriate data type for the field, using Table AC-5 as a reference
- ☐ To specify how the data should be formatted, click the appropriate property box in the Field Properties pane, then make the modifications using Table AC-6 as a reference
- ☐ Select the field(s) to be defined as the primary key, click **Edit** on the menu bar, then click **Primary Key**

Button Method

- ☐ Click the **Tables button** [Tables] on the Objects bar, then click the **Design button** [Design] on the Database window toolbar
- ☐ Follow the steps in the third through fifth bullets of the Create Tables Using Table Design View Menu Method above
- ☐ Click the **Primary Key button** [ ] on the Table Design toolbar

Table AC-5 Data Type Options

Data type	Description of data
Text	Text, combinations of text and numbers, or formatted numbers such as phone numbers
Memo	Text longer than 255 characters
Number	Numeric information to be used in calculations
Date/Time	Dates and times
Currency	Monetary values
AutoNumber	Integers assigned by Access to sequentially order each record added to a table
Yes/No	Only two values (Yes/No, On/Off, True/False) can be chosen for this type of field
OLE Object	Files created in other programs (OLE stands for Object Linking and Embedding)
Hyperlink	Links to Web page addresses, files, or objects

Table AC-6 Field Properties

Field property	Can be used to	Used for data type(s):
Field Size	Set the maximum size for data stored in a field set	Text, Number, and AutoNumber
Format	Customize the way numbers, dates, times, and text are displayed and printed, or use special symbols to create custom formats, such as to display information in all uppercase	Text, Memo, Date/Time, AutoNumber, Yes/No, Hyperlink, and Number
Decimal Places	Specify the number of decimal places that are displayed, but not how many decimal places are stored	Number and Currency
Input Mask	Make data entry easier and to control the values users can enter in a text box control, such as (___) ___-____ for a phone number	Text and Date
Caption	Provide helpful information to the user through captions on objects in various views	All fields

Table AC-6 Field Properties (continued)

Field property	Can be used to	Used for data type(s):
Default Value	Specify a value that is entered in a field automatically when a new record is added. For example, in an Addresses table you can set the default value for the State field to Massachusetts. When a new record is added to the table, you can either accept this value or enter a new state	All fields except AutoNumber or OLE object
Validation Rule	Specify requirements for data entered into a record, field, or control	All fields except AutoNumber OLE object
Validation Text	When data is entered that violates the Validation Rule setting, you can use the Validation Text property to specify the message to be displayed to the user	All fields where a Validation Rule is specified
Required	Specify whether a value is required in a field	All fields except AutoNumber
Indexed	Set a single-field index that will speed up queries on the indexed fields as well as sorting and grouping operations	Text, Number, Date/Time, Currency, AutoNumber, and Yes/No, Hyperlink, and Memo

ADD A PRE-DEFINED INPUT MASK TO A FIELD

Wizard Method

☐ Open the table in Design View
☐ Select the appropriate field, then click the **Input Mask property box** in the Field Properties pane
☐ Click the **Build button** [...], then click **Yes** if prompted to save the table
☐ Navigate through the Input Mask Wizard, making changes or accepting the defaults as appropriate to create the Input Mask, then click **Finish**

CREATE LOOKUP FIELDS

Menu Method

☐ Open the table in Design View, then click a blank field
☐ Click **Insert** on the menu bar, then click **Lookup Field**
☐ Navigate through the Lookup Wizard, making changes or accepting the defaults as appropriate to create the Lookup field, then click **Finish**

Button Method

☐ Open the table in Design View, then click a blank field
☐ In the Data Type column, click the appropriate cell, click the **list arrow**, then click **Lookup Wizard**
☐ Navigate through the Lookup Wizard, making changes or accepting the defaults as appropriate to create the Lookup field, then click **Finish**

MODIFY FIELD PROPERTIES

Button Method

☐ Open the table in Design View
☐ To modify the type of data, click the Data Type field, click the **Data Type list arrow**, then click the appropriate data type for the field, using Table AC-5 as a reference
☐ To modify how the data should be formatted, click the appropriate property box in the Field Properties pane, then make the modifications using Table AC-6 as a reference

ACCESS SKILL SET 3: CREATING AND MODIFYING QUERIES

CREATE AND MODIFY SELECT QUERIES

Create Select Queries Using the Simple Query Wizard

Menu Method

- ☐ Click **Insert** on the menu bar, then click **Query**
- ☐ In the New Query dialog box, click **Simple Query Wizard**, then click **OK**
- ☐ Navigate through the Simple Query Wizard, making changes or accepting the defaults as appropriate to create the form, then click **Finish**

Button Method

- ☐ Click the **Queries button** [⬚ Queries] on the Objects bar, then double-click **Create query by using wizard**
- ☐ Follow the steps in the third bullet of the Create and Modify Select Queries Menu Method above

Create Select Queries Using Query Design View

Menu Method

- ☐ Click **Insert** on the menu bar, then click **Query**
- ☐ In the New Query dialog box, click **Design View**, then click **OK**
- ☐ In the Show Table dialog box, click each object to query, clicking **Add** after each, then click **Close**
- ☐ Move the fields into the query design grid by clicking fields from the objects in the upper pane and dragging them to the appropriate column in the bottom pane
- ☐ For each field you want to specify a sort order, click the **cell**, click the **list arrow**, then click the sort order
- ☐ Click **Query** on the menu bar, then click **Run**

Button Method

- ☐ Click the **Queries button** [⬚ Queries] on the Objects bar, then click the **New button** [⬚] on the Database window toolbar
- ☐ In the New Query dialog box, click **Design View**, then click **OK**
- ☐ Follow the steps in the third through fifth bullets in the Create Select Queries Using Query Design View Menu Method above
- ☐ Click the **Run button** [⬚] on the Query Design toolbar

ADD CALCULATED FIELDS TO SELECT QUERIES

Add a Calculated Field Using Query Design View

Keyboard Method

- ☐ Open the query in Design View
- ☐ Click the appropriate Field cell in the query design grid, then type the formula

  OR

☐ Open the query in Design View
☐ Right-click the appropriate Field cell in the Query Design grid, then click **Zoom** on the shortcut menu
☐ In the Zoom dialog box, type the formula, then click **OK**

FORMAT VALUES IN A CALCULATED FIELD

Menu Method

☐ Open the query in Design View
☐ Right-click the appropriate field, then click **Properties** on the shortcut menu
☐ In the Field Properties dialog box, click the **General tab** if necessary
☐ Click the **Format property box**, click the **Format property list arrow**, then click the appropriate property
☐ Click the Field Properties dialog box **Close button**

Button Method

☐ Open the query in Design View
☐ Click the field name, then click the **Properties button** on the Query Design toolbar
☐ Follow the steps in the third through fifth bullets in the Format Values in a Calculated Field Menu Method above

Keyboard Method

☐ Open the query in Design View
☐ Click the field name, then press **[Alt][Enter]**
☐ Follow the steps in the third through fifth bullets in the Format Values in a Calculated Field Menu Method above

ACCESS SKILL SET 4: CREATING AND MODIFYING FORMS

CREATE AND DISPLAY FORMS

Create Forms Using AutoForms

Menu Method
☐ Click **Insert** on the menu bar, then click **Form**
☐ In the New Form dialog box, click an appropriate **AutoForm**
☐ Click the **Choose the table or query where the object's data comes from list arrow**, click the appropriate object, then click **OK**

Button Method
☐ Double-click the object in the Database window
☐ Click the **New Object list arrow** 🔳 ▾ on the Database toolbar, then click **AutoForm**

Create Forms Using the Form Wizard

Menu Method
☐ Click **Insert** on the menu bar, then click **Form**
☐ In the New Form dialog box, click **Form Wizard**
☐ Click the **Choose the table or query where the object's data comes from list arrow**, click the appropriate object, then click **OK**
☐ Navigate through the Form Wizard, making changes or accepting the defaults as appropriate to create the form, then click **Finish**

Button Method
☐ Click the **Forms button** 🔳 Forms on the Objects bar, then double-click **Create form by using wizard**
☐ Follow the steps in the fourth bullet in the Create Forms Using the Form Wizard Menu Method above

MODIFY FORM PROPERTIES

Apply an AutoFormat to a Form

Button Method
☐ Open the form in Design View
☐ Click the **AutoFormat button** 🔳 on the Form Design toolbar
☐ In the AutoFormat dialog box, click the appropriate option(s), then click **OK**

Modify a Control on a Form

☐ Open the form in Design View
☐ Select the control to be modified
☐ Use Table AC-7 as a reference to modify the control appropriately
☐ Use the pointers described in Table AC-8 to move or resize a control

Table AC-7 Common Formatting Effects

Formatting (Form/Report) toolbar buttons	Effect
Arial	Font
10	Font Size
B	Bold
I	Italic
U	Underline
≣	Align Left
≣	Center
≣	Align Right
⬠ ▾	Fill/Back Color
A ▾	Font/Fore Color
✐ ▾	Line/Border Color
▢ ▾	Line/Border Width
▱ ▾	Special Effect

Table AC-8 Form Design View Pointer Shapes

Shape	When does this shape appear?	Action
↖	Appears by default when you point to any control on the form which is not selected	Single-click to select a control
✋	When you point to a selected control's edge (not to a sizing handle or the move handle)	Drag to move the selected control(s)
☝	When you point to a selected control's move handle in the upper-left corner	Drag to move only the control where pointer is currently positioned, but not other selected controls
↔ ↕ ⤢ ⤡	When you point to a sizing handle	Drag to resize a control; double-click to resize the control to fit the text

ACCESS SKILL SET 5: VIEWING AND ORGANIZING INFORMATION

ENTER, EDIT, AND DELETE RECORDS

Enter, Edit, and Delete Records in Datasheet View or Form View

Menu Method

☐ Open the table in Table Datasheet or Form View

☐ Right-click any record selector button, then click New Record or Delete Record from the shortcut menu

Button and Keyboard Methods

Open the table in Table Datasheet or Form View, then use Tables AC-9 and AC-10 as a reference to edit and navigate the records.

Table AC-9 Methods for Entering and Editing Data

Action	Keyboard	Button	Mode/View Available
Inserts a new record in the database		New Record button	Navigation mode
Deletes a record from the database	[Delete]	Delete Record button	Navigation mode
Moves to the next field	[Tab]		
Deletes one character to the left of the insertion point	[Backspace]		Edit mode
Deletes one character to the right of the insertion point	[Delete]		Edit mode
Toggles between Edit and Navigation mode	[F2]		
Undoes the change to the current field	[Esc]	Undo button	
Undoes all changes to the current record	[Esc][Esc]		Datasheet view
Starts the Spell Check feature	[F7]	Spelling button	
Inserts the value from the same field in the previous record into the current field	[Ctrl][']		
Inserts the current date in a date field	[Ctrl][;]		

Table AC-10 Navigation Toolbar Buttons

Button	Name
⏮	First Record button
◀	Previous Record button
▶	Next Record button
⏭	Last Record button
▶*	New Record button

CREATE CROSSTAB QUERIES

Menu Method
☐ Click **Insert** on the menu bar, then click **Query**
☐ In the New Query dialog box, click **Crosstab Query Wizard**, then click **OK**
☐ Navigate through the Crosstab Query Wizard, making changes or accepting the defaults as appropriate to create the query, then click **Finish**
   Note: to create a Select Query, see Create and Modify a Select Query in Skill Set 3

Button Method
☐ Click the **Queries button** | 🗗 Queries | on the Objects bar
☐ Click the **New button** 🗗 on the Database window toolbar
☐ In the New Query dialog box, double-click **Crosstab Query Wizard**
☐ Follow the third bullet in the Create Crosstab Queries Menu Method above

SORT RECORDS

Sort Records in Datasheet View

Menu Method
☐ Open the table or query in Datasheet View
☐ Click any value in the field by which to sort
☐ Click **Records** on the menu bar, point to **Sort**, then select the appropriate sort option

Button Method
☐ Open the table or query in Datasheet View
☐ Click any value in the field by which to sort
☐ Click the **Sort Descending button** 🔽 or the the **Sort Ascending button** 🔼 on the Datasheet toolbar

Sort Records in Query Design View

Button Method
☐ Open the query in Design View
☐ Click the **Sort cell** for the field by which to sort, click the **list arrow**, then click **Ascending** or **Descending**

FILTER RECORDS

Filter Records Using Filter by Selection

Menu Method

☐ Open the table or query in Datasheet View
☐ Click any value in the column by which to filter
☐ Click **Records** on the menu bar, point to **Filter**, then click **Filter by Selection**

Button Method

☐ Open the table or query in Datasheet View
☐ Click any value in the column by which to filter
☐ Click the **Filter By Selection button** on the Datasheet toolbar

Filter Records Using Filter by Form

Menu Method

☐ Open the table or query in Datasheet View
☐ Click **Records** on the menu bar, point to **Filter**, then click **Filter by Form**
☐ Click the cell that contains the value by which to filter, then type the criteria using Table AC-11 as a reference, or click the cell by which to sort, click the **list arrow**, then click the value by which to filter
☐ Click **Filter** on the menu bar, then click **Apply Filter/Sort**

Button Method

☐ Open the table or query in Datasheet View
☐ Click the **Filter By Form button** on the Filter/Sort toolbar
☐ Click the cell that contains the value by which to filter, type the filter criteria using Table AC-11 as a reference, or click the cell by which to sort, click the **list arrow**, then click the value by which to filter
☐ Click the **Apply Filter button** on the Filter/Sort toolbar

Table AC-11 Comparison Operators

Operator	Description	Expression	Meaning
<	Less than	<"Cassidy"	Names from A through Cassidy, but not Cassidy
<=	Less than or equal to	<="Delaney"	Names from A through, and including, Delaney
>	Greater than	>450	Numbers greater than 450
>=	Greater than or equal to	>=450	Numbers greater than or equal to 450
<>	Not equal to	<>"Malone"	Any name except for Malone
OR	Needs to meet 1 of 2 criteria	"Murphy" OR "Malone"	Only names Murphy and Malone
AND	Needs to meet both of 2 criteria	>="Cassidy" AND <="Murphy"	All names between and including Cassidy and Murphy

Access Skill Set 6: Defining Relationships

Create One-to-Many Relationships

Menu Method

☐ Click **Tools** on the menu bar, then click **Relationships**, or right-click the database window, then click **Relationships** on the shortcut menu
☐ In the Relationships window, click **Relationships** on the menu bar, then click **Show Table** to display the Show Table dialog box if necessary
☐ In the Show Table dialog box, click the object(s) to include, clicking **Add** after each, then click **Close**
☐ Drag the field from field list it appears in to one you want it to relate to you want to create the relationship from its field list to the field list to which you want to relate it
☐ In the Edit Relationships dialog box, click **Create**
☐ Click **File** on the menu bar, then click **Save**

Button Method

☐ Click the **Relationships button** 🔲 on the Database toolbar
☐ In the Relationships window, click the **Show Table button** 🔲 to display the Show Table dialog box if necessary
☐ Follow the steps in the third through fifth bullets in the Create One-to-Many Relationships Menu Method above
☐ Click the **Save button** on the Relationships toolbar

Enforce Referential Integrity

Menu Method

☐ Click **Tools** on the menu bar, then click **Relationships**, or right-click the database window, then click **Relationships** on the shortcut menu
☐ Double-click the relationship you want to enforce referential integrity
☐ In the Edit Relationships dialog box, click the **Enforce Referential Integrity check box** to select it, then click **OK**

Button Method

☐ Click the **Relationships button** 🔲 on the Database toolbar to open the Relationships window
☐ Follow the steps in the second and third bullets of the Enforce Referential Integrity Menu Method above

ACCESS SKILL SET 7: PRODUCING REPORTS

CREATE AND FORMAT REPORTS

Create Reports Using the Report Wizard

Menu Method

- ☐ Click **Insert** on the menu bar, then click **Report**
- ☐ In the New Report dialog box, click **Report Wizard**, then click **OK**
- ☐ Navigate through the Report Wizard, making changes or accepting the defaults as appropriate to create the report, then click **Finish**

Button Method

- ☐ Click the **Reports button** [🔲 Reports] on the Objects bar, then double-click **Create report by using wizard**
- ☐ Follow the steps in the third bullet of the Create Reports Using the Report Wizard Menu Method above

Format Reports Using Report Design View

Button Method

- ☐ Open the report in Report Design View
- ☐ Click the appropriate **control**
- ☐ Modify the control, using Table AC-4 as a reference

ADD CALCULATED CONTROLS TO REPORTS

Add Subtotals for Groups of Records

Button Method

- ☐ Open the report in Report Design View
- ☐ Click the **Text Box button** [abl] on the Toolbox toolbar, then create a text box on the form to hold the subtotal
- ☐ Click the **Properties button** [🔲] on the Report Design toolbar
- ☐ In the Text Box property window, click the **Control Source property box**, then click the **Build button** [...]
- ☐ In the Expression Builder dialog box, enter the formula, then click **OK**
- ☐ Click the Text Box property window **Close button**

Add Date Calculated Controls

Menu Method

- ☐ Open the report in Design View
- ☐ Click **Insert** on the menu bar, then click **Date and Time**
- ☐ Select the appropriate options in the Date and Time dialog box, then click **OK**
- ☐ Place the date text box in an appropriate location on the report

Button Method

- ☐ Open the report in Design View
- ☐ Click the **Text Box button** 🔲 on the Toolbox toolbar, then click the report where the date should appear
- ☐ Click **Unbound** in the new text box, type **=Date()**, then press **[Enter]**

PREVIEW AND PRINT REPORTS

Preview a Report

Menu Method

- ☐ Click the **Reports button** 🔲 Reports on the Objects bar
- ☐ Click the report to preview
- ☐ Click **File** on the menu bar, then click **Print Preview**

  OR

- ☐ Click the **Reports button** 🔲 Reports on the Objects bar
- ☐ Right-click the report to preview
- ☐ Click **Print Preview** on the shortcut menu

Button Method

- ☐ Click the **Reports button** 🔲 Reports on the Objects bar, click the report to preview, then click the **Preview button** 🔲 Preview on the Database window toolbar

  OR

- ☐ Click the **Reports button** 🔲 Reports on the Objects bar, click the report to preview, then click the **Print Preview button** 🔲 on the Standard Buttons toolbar

  OR

- ☐ Click the **Reports button** 🔲 Reports on the Objects bar, then double-click the report

Print a Report

Menu Method

- ☐ Click the **Reports button** 🔲 Reports on the Objects bar
- ☐ Click the report to print
- ☐ Click **File** on the menu bar, click **Print**, then click **OK** in the Print dialog box

  OR

- ☐ Click the **Reports button** 🔲 Reports on the Objects bar
- ☐ Right-click the report
- ☐ Click **Print** on the shortcut menu

Button Method

- ☐ Click the **Reports button** 🔲 Reports on the Objects bar
- ☐ Click the report to print
- ☐ Click the **Print button** 🖨 on the Standard Buttons toolbar

ACCESS SKILL SET 8: INTEGRATING WITH OTHER APPLICATIONS

IMPORT DATA TO ACCESS

Import Data from an Excel Workbook

Menu Method
- ☐ Click **File** on the menu bar, point to **Get External Data**, then click **Import**
- ☐ In the Import dialog box, navigate to the appropriate drive and folder, click the **Files of type list arrow**, click **Microsoft Excel**, click the filename, then click **Import**
- ☐ Navigate through the Import Spreadsheet Wizard, making changes or accepting the defaults as appropriate to create the database, click **Finish**
- ☐ Click **OK** in the message box

Button Method
- ☐ Click the **New button** 🔲 on the Database window toolbar
- ☐ In the New Table dialog box, click **Import Table**, then click **OK**
- ☐ Follow the steps in the second through fourth bullets in the Import Data From an Excel Workbook Menu Method above

Import Objects from Another Access Database

Menu Method
- ☐ Click **File** on the menu bar, point to **Get External Data**, then click **Import**
- ☐ In the Import dialog box, navigate to the appropriate drive and folder, click the **Files of type list arrow**, click **Microsoft Access** if necessary, click the **filename**, then click **Import**
- ☐ In the Import Objects dialog box, click the appropriate tab(s), then click the appropriate object(s)
- ☐ Click **OK** to import the object(s) from the source database to the destination database

EXPORT DATA FROM ACCESS

Export Data to an Excel Workbook

Menu Method
- ☐ Select the appropriate object button on the Objects bar to select the table or query, then click the object to export
- ☐ Click **File** on the menu bar, then click **Export**
- ☐ In the Export dialog box, navigate to the appropriate drive and folder, click the **Save as type list arrow**, click **Microsoft Excel 97-2002**, then click **Export**

Button Method
- ☐ Select the appropriate object button on the Objects bar to select the table or query, then click the object to export
- ☐ Click the **OfficeLinks list arrow** 📊▾ on the Database toolbar, then click **Analyze It with Microsoft Excel**

Export Data to a Web Page

Menu Method

☐ Click the **Reports button** 🔳 Reports on the Objects bar, then click the report to export

☐ Click **File** on the menu bar, then click **Export**

☐ In the Export Report dialog box, navigate to the appropriate drive and folder, click the **Save as type list arrow**, click **HTML Documents**, then click **Export**

☐ Click **OK** in the HTML Output Options dialog box

CREATE A SIMPLE DATA ACCESS PAGE

Create a Data Access Page for Data Entry

Menu Method

☐ Click **Insert** on the menu bar, then click **Page**

☐ In the New Data Access Page dialog box, click **Page Wizard**, then click **OK**

☐ Navigate through the Page Wizard, making changes or accepting the defaults as appropriate to create the data access page, then click **Finish**

Wizard Method

☐ Click the **Pages button** 🔳 Pages on the Objects bar, then double-click **Create data access page by using wizard**

☐ Follow the steps in the third bullet in the Create a Data Access Page for Data Entry Menu method above

Create a Data Access Page for Data Reporting

Menu Method

☐ Click **Insert** on the menu bar, then click **Page**

☐ In the New Data Access Page dialog box, click **Page Wizard**, then click **OK**

☐ Navigate through the Page Wizard, making changes or accepting the defaults as appropriate to create the data access page, then click **Finish**

Wizard Method

☐ Click the **Pages button** 🔳 Pages on the Objects bar, then double-click **Create data access page by using wizard**

☐ Follow the steps in the third bullet in the Create a Data Access Page for Data Reporting Menu method above

ACCESS **EXPERT** EXAM REFERENCE

Skill Sets:

9 Creating and modifying tables
10 Creating and modifying forms
11 Refining queries
12 Producing reports
13 Defining relationships
14 Operating Access on the Web
15 Using Access tools
16 Creating database applications

ACCESS SKILL SET 9: CREATING AND MODIFYING TABLES

USE DATA VALIDATION

Keyboard Method

☐ Open the table in Design View
☐ Click the field to validate
☐ Click the **Validation Rule property box** in the Field Properties pane, then type the validation criteria
☐ Click the Validation Text property box
☐ Type the error message in the Validation Text property box

LINK TABLES

Menu Method

☐ Click **File** on the menu bar, point to **Get External Data**, then click **Link Tables**
☐ In the Link dialog box, click the **Look in list arrow**, navigate to the appropriate drive and folder, click the database, then click **Link**
☐ In the Link Tables dialog box, click the table to which to link
☐ Click **OK**

CREATE LOOKUP FIELDS AND MODIFY LOOKUP FIELD PROPERTIES

Create Lookup Fields

Menu Method

☐ Open the table in Design View
☐ Click **Insert** on the menu bar, then click **Lookup Field**
☐ Navigate through the Lookup Wizard, making changes or accepting the defaults to create the Lookup field as appropriate, then click **Finish**

☐ Click **Yes** if prompted to save the file

OR

☐ Open the table in Table Design View
☐ Click the Data Type cell for the field for which you want to create a lookup, click the **list arrow**, then click **Lookup Wizard**
☐ Follow the third and fourth bullets in the Create Lookup Fields Menu Method above

Modify Lookup Properties

Menu Method

☐ Open the table in Design View
☐ Click the Lookup field to modify, then click the **Lookup tab** in the Field Properties pane
☐ Click the **Row Source property box**, then modify the entry

Button Method

☐ Follow the first and second bullets in the Modify Lookup Properties Menu Method above
☐ Click the **Row Source property box**, then click the **Build button** ⬚
☐ In the Query Builder window, modify the query, then click the **Close button**

CREATE AND MODIFY INPUT MASKS

Create Input Masks

Menu Method

☐ Open the table in Table Design View
☐ Click the field to modify, click the **General tab** in the Field Properties pane if necessary, then click the **Input Mask property box**
☐ Click the **Build button** ⬚, then click **Yes** if prompted to save the table
☐ Navigate through the Input Mask Wizard, making changes or accepting the defaults to create the Input Mask as appropriate, then click **Finish**

Modify Input Masks

Menu Method

☐ Open the table in Table Design View
☐ Click the field to modify, click the **General tab** in the Field Properties pane if necessary, then click the **Input Mask property box**
☐ Modify the Input Mask as appropriate using Table AC-12 as a reference

Table AC-12 The Parts of the Input Mask Entry

Part	Description	Options	Examples (parts appear in bold)	How a sample entry appears in Datasheet View or Form View
First	Controls display of and data type that can be entered	9: an optional number 0: a required number ?: an optional letter L: a required letter \: the next character will display as entered	Telephone Number \(999\)\-000\-0000;1;*	(978)-555-7000 OR ( ) 555-7000
Second	Establishes whether all displayed characters (such as slashes in the Date field) are stored in the field, or just the part you type	0: stores all characters 1: stores only typed characters	Zip Code 00000\-9999;0;_	56178- OR 56178-7157
Third	Establishes the placeholder character that will display to represent characters that will be typed in a field	* (asterisk) _ (underscore) # (pound sign)	Social Security Number 000\-00\-0000;0;#	Before typing appears as: ###-##-#### After typing appears as: 555-44-1111

ACCESS SKILL SET 10: CREATING AND MODIFYING FORMS

CREATE A FORM IN DESIGN VIEW

Menu Method

☐ Open a new form in Design View
☐ Click **View** on the menu bar, then click **Properties** or right-click, then click **Properties** on the shortcut menu
☐ On the Form property sheet, click the **Data tab** if necessary
☐ Click the **Record Source list arrow**, then click the appropriate source object
☐ Click **View** on the menu bar, then click **Properties** to close the property sheet
☐ Drag each field from the source object window to the appropriate location on the form

Button Method

☐ Open a new form in Design View
☐ Click the **Properties button** 🔲 on the Form Design toolbar to open the Form property sheet, then click the **Data tab** if necessary
☐ Click the **Record Source list arrow**, then click the appropriate source object
☐ Click the **Properties button** 🔲 to close the property sheet
☐ Drag each field from the source object window to the appropriate location on the form

Keyboard Method

☐ Open a new form in Design View
☐ Press **[F4]** to open the Form property sheet, then click the **Data tab** if necessary
☐ Click the **Record Source list arrow**, then click the appropriate source object
☐ Click the **Properties button** 🔲 to close the property sheet
☐ Drag each field from the source object window to the appropriate location on the form

CREATE A SWITCHBOARD AND SET STARTUP OPTIONS

Create a Switchboard

Menu Method

☐ Click **Tools** on the menu bar, point to **Database Utilities**, then click **Switchboard Manager**
☐ Click **Yes** if prompted to create a switchboard
☐ In the Switchboard Manager dialog box, click **Edit**, then click **New** in the Edit Switchboard Page dialog box
☐ In the Edit Switchboard Item dialog box, select a switchboard, select the appropriate options, then click **OK**

□ When finished making modifications, click **Close** in the Edit Switchboard Page dialog box, then click **Close** in the Switchboard Manager dialog box

Modify a Switchboard

Menu Method

□ Click **Tools** on the menu bar, point to **Database Utilities**, then click **Switchboard Manager**
□ In the Switchboard Manager dialog box, click the appropriate Switchboard page, then click **Edit**
□ Click the item to modify in the Edit Switchboard Page dialog box, then use Table AC-13 to modify the text

Table AC-13   Edit Switchboard Page Dialog Box Buttons

Button	Function
New	Create a new switchboard item
Edit	Edit a switchboard item
Delete	Delete a switchboard item
Move Up	Move to a higher location on the switchboard
Move Down	Move to a lower location on the switchboard

Set Startup Options

Menu Method

□ Click **Tools** on the menu bar, then click **Startup**
□ In the Startup dialog box, click the appropriate option(s), using Table AC-14 as a reference
□ Click **OK**

Table AC-14   Startup Options

Option	Description
Application Title	Instead of the database name, displays text entered in the Database title bar
Application Icon	Displays an icon or bitmap image to the left of the text in the title bars
Menu Bar	Determines which menu bar appears when the database is opened
Allow Full Menus	Allows or disallows use of full menus
Allow Default Shortcut Menus	Allows or disallows use of shortcut menus
Use Access Special Keys	Allows or disallows ability to work with special keys such as the function keys
Display Form/Page	Determines a form or page object to appear when the database is opened

Table AC-14 Startup Options (continued)

Option	Description
Display Database Window	Allows or disallows ability to display the Database window
Display Status Bar	Allows or disallows ability to display the status bar
Shortcut Menu Bar	Establishes which menu bar appears when you right-click a menu bar
Allow Built-in Toolbars	Displays or hides toolbars
Allow Toolbar/Menu Changes	Allows or disallows modification of toolbars and menu bars

ADD SUBFORM CONTROLS TO ACCESS FORMS

Button Method

☐ Open the form in Design View

☐ Click the **Subform/Subreport button** 🔲 on the Toolbox toolbar, then click the location on the form where you want to add the control

☐ If the SubForm Wizard does not open, press **[Ctrl][Z]** to delete the SubForm you just created, click the **Control Wizards button** 🔲 on the Toolbox toolbar, click the **Subform/Subreport button** 🔲 on the Toolbox toolbar then click the location on the **?** where you want to add the control

☐ Navigate through the SubForm Wizard, making changes or accepting the defaults to create the SubForm as appropriate, then click **Finish**

ACCESS SKILL SET 11: REFINING QUERIES

SPECIFY MULTIPLE QUERY CRITERIA

Use AND Conditions

Menu Method

- ☐ Open a new query in Design View
- ☐ Click **Query** on the menu bar, then click **Show Table** to open the Show Table dialog box if necessary
- ☐ In the Show Table dialog box, click the appropriate table(s) and/or query(ies), clicking **Add** after each, then click **Close**
- ☐ Drag at least two fields from the Category field list to the appropriate column of the query design grid
- ☐ Click the **Criteria cell** for each field, then type the criteria

Use OR Conditions

Menu Method

- ☐ Open a new query in Design View
- ☐ Click **Query** on the menu bar, then click **Show Table** to open the Show Table dialog box if necessary
- ☐ In the Show Table dialog box, click the appropriate table(s) and/or query(ies), clicking **Add** after each, then click **Close**
- ☐ Drag at least two fields from the Category field list to the appropriate column of the query design grid
- ☐ Click the **Criteria cell** for the first field, then type the criteria
- ☐ Click the **Or cell** (the Criteria cell in the second row) for the next field, then type the criteria

CREATE AND APPLY ADVANCED FILTERS

Menu Method

- ☐ Open the Table in Table Datasheet View, click **Records** on the menu bar, point to **Filter**, then click **Advanced Filter/Sort**
- ☐ Double-click each field to add in the appropriate order
- ☐ Click the **Criteria cell** for each field, then type the criteria
- ☐ Click the **Sort cell** for each field, click the **list arrow**, then click **Ascending** or **Descending**
- ☐ Click **Filter** on the menu bar, then click **Apply Filter/Sort**

Button Method

- ☐ Follow the first through fourth bullets in the Create and Apply Advanced Filters Menu Method above
- ☐ Click the **Apply Filter button** 🟦 on the Filter/Sort toolbar

CREATE AND RUN PARAMETER QUERIES

Menu Method

- ☐ Open the query in Design View

☐ Click the criteria cell, then type the parameter criteria, using **[** and **]** (left and right brackets) at the beginning and end of the parameters
☐ Switch to Datasheet View
☐ Type the parameter in the Enter Parameter Value dialog box, then click **OK**

CREATE AND RUN ACTION QUERIES

Menu Method

☐ Open a new query in Design View
☐ Click **Query** on the menu bar, then click **Show Table** to open the Show Table dialog box if necessary
☐ In the Show Table dialog box, click the appropriate table(s) and/or query(ies), clicking **Add** after each, then click **Close**
☐ Click **Query** on the menu bar, then click the appropriate query type, using Table AC-15 as a reference
☐ Click the **Criteria cell** for the field, then type the criteria
☐ Click **Query** on the menu bar, click **Run**, then click **Yes** in the message box

Button Method

☐ Open a new query in Design View
☐ Click the **Show Table button** 🖳 on the Query Design toolbar to open the Show Table dialog box if necessary
☐ In the Show Table dialog box, click the appropriate table(s) and/or query(ies), clicking **Add** after each, then click **Close**
☐ Click the **Query Type list arrow** 🗗▾, then click the appropriate query type, using Table AC-15 as a reference
☐ Click the **Criteria cell** for the field, then type the criteria
☐ Click the **Run button** ⏸ on the Query Design toolbar, then click **Yes** in the message box

Table AC-15 Action Queries

Type of action query	Query icon	Used for	You need to
Make-Table	🖳❗	Creating a new table using data in another table(s)	Enter the table name in the Make Table dialog box, then click OK
Update	🖉❗	Making global changes to record(s) in table(s)	Click the Update To property box, then select a location
Append	⊕❗	Adding record(s) from a table(s) to the end of a table	Enter the table name in the Append dialog box, then click OK
Delete	✗❗	Deleting record(s) from table(s)	Click the Delete property box list arrow, then click Where or From

USE AGGREGATE FUNCTIONS IN QUERIES

Button Method

☐ Open the query in Design View

☐ Click the **Totals button** ∑ on the Query Design toolbar to display the Total row in the query design grid

☐ Click **Group By** in the Total row for the field, click the **Group By list arrow**, then click the appropriate option, using Table AC-16 as a reference

Table AC-16 Aggregate Functions

Function	Used to calculate the	Used for field types
Sum	Total value	Number, Date/Time, Currency, and AutoNumber
Avg	Average value	Number, Date/Time, Currency, and AutoNumber
Min	Lowest value in a field	Text, Number, Date/Time, Currency, and AutoNumber
Max	Highest value in a field	Text, Number, Date/Time, Currency, and AutoNumber
Count	Number of values in a field (not counting null values)	Text, Memo, Number, Date/Time, Currency, AutoNumber, Yes/No, and OLE Object
StDev	Standard deviation of values	Number, Date/Time, Currency, and AutoNumber
Var	Variance of values	Number, Date/Time, Currency, and AutoNumber

Access Skill Set 12: Producing Reports

Create and Modify Reports

Create and Modify a Report in Report Design View

Menu Method

- ☐ Open a new report in Report Design View
- ☐ Click **View** on the menu bar, then click **Properties** or right-click, then click **Properties** on the shortcut menu
- ☐ On the Report property sheet, click the **Data tab** if necessary, click the **Record Source list arrow**, then click the source
- ☐ Click **View** on the menu bar, then click **Properties** to close the property sheet
- ☐ Drag the field(s) to the appropriate section(s) of the form
- ☐ Add other objects as necessary to complete the report, then make your modifications

Button Method

- ☐ Open a new report in Design View
- ☐ Click the **Properties button** 🔲 on the Report Design toolbar
- ☐ On the Report property sheet, click the **Data tab** if necessary, click the **Record Source list arrow**, then click the source
- ☐ Click the **Properties button** 🔲 to close the property sheet
- ☐ Drag the field(s) to the appropriate section(s) of the form
- ☐ Add other objects as necessary to complete the report, then make your modifications

Keyboard Method

- ☐ Open a new report in Report Design View
- ☐ Press **[F4]**
- ☐ On the Report property sheet, click the **Data tab** if necessary, click the **Record Source list arrow**, then click the source
- ☐ Click the **Properties button** 🔲 to close the property sheet
- ☐ Drag the field(s) to the appropriate section(s) of the form
- ☐ Add other objects as necessary to complete the report, then make your modifications

Add SubReport Controls to Access Reports

Menu Method

- ☐ Open the report in Design View
- ☐ Click the **Subform/Subreport button** 🔲 on the Toolbox toolbar, then click where you want to add controls

☐ If the SubReport Wizard does not open, click the **Control Wizards button** on the Toolbox toolbar, click the **Subform/Subreport button** on the Toolbox toolbar, then click where you want to add controls

☐ Navigate through the SubReport Wizard, making changes or accepting the defaults to create the SubReport as appropriate, then click **Finish**

SORT AND GROUP DATA IN REPORTS

Menu Method

☐ Open the report in Design View
☐ Click **View** on the menu bar, then click **Sorting and Grouping**
☐ Select the appropriate options in the Sorting and Grouping dialog box, then click the **Close button**

Button Method

☐ Open the report in Design View
☐ Click the **Sorting and Grouping button** on the Report Design toolbar
☐ Select the appropriate options in the Sorting and Grouping dialog box, then click the **Close button**

ACCESS SKILL SET 13: DEFINING RELATIONSHIPS

ESTABLISH ONE-TO-MANY RELATIONSHIPS

Menu Method
- [ ] Click **Tools** on the menu bar, then click **Relationships**
- [ ] If necessary, click **Relationships** on the menu bar, then click **Show Table** to display the Show Table dialog box
- [ ] In the Show Table dialog box, click each table or query to include, clicking **Add** after each, then click **Close** in the Show Table dialog box
- [ ] Drag the field which you want to relate from its field list, to the same field in the field list to which you want to relate it
- [ ] In the Edit Relationships dialog box, make the appropriate selections, then click **Create**

Button Method
- [ ] Click the **Relationships button** [icon] on the Database toolbar to open the Relationships window
- [ ] If necessary, click the **Show Table button** [icon] on the Relationship toolbar to display the Show Table dialog box
- [ ] Follow the third through fifth bullets in the Establish One-to-Many Relationships Menu Method above

ESTABLISH MANY-TO-MANY RELATIONSHIPS

Menu Method
- [ ] Choose two unrelated tables for which you want to establish a many-to-many relationship
- [ ] Open a new table in Table Design View to create a junction table to join the two tables
- [ ] Create a foreign key field to serve as the "many" side of a "one-to-many" link for each of the original tables
- [ ] Click the field to be the primary key, click **Edit** on the menu bar, then click **Primary Key**
- [ ] Click **File** on the menu bar, then click **Save**
- [ ] In the Save As dialog box, type the table name in the Table Name text box, click **OK**, then close Table Design View
- [ ] Click **Tools** on the menu bar, then click **Relationships**
- [ ] If necessary, in the Relationships window, click **Relationships** on the menu bar, then click **Show Table** to display the Show Table dialog box
- [ ] In the Show Table dialog box, click the two original tables and the new junction table, clicking **Add** after each, then click **Close** in the Show Table dialog box
- [ ] Create one-to-many relationships between the two original tables and the junction table by dragging the primary key field from the original table to the foreign key field of the junction table
- [ ] In the Edit Relationship dialog box, make the appropriate selections, then click **Create**

Button Method

☐ Follow the first through third bullets in Establish Many-to-Many Relationships mentioned above

☐ Click the field to be the primary key, then click the **Primary Key button** 🔑 on the Table Design toolbar

☐ Click the **Save button** 🖫 on the Table Design toolbar

☐ In the Save As dialog box, type the table name in the Table Name text box, click **OK**, then close Table Design View

☐ Click the **Relationships button** 🔡 on the Database toolbar

☐ If necessary, in the Relationships window, click the **Show Table button** 🔡 on the Relationship toolbar to display the Show Table dialog box

☐ Follow the ninth through eleventh bullets in the Establish Many-to-Many Relationships Menu Method above

Access Skill Set 14: Operating Access on the Web

Create and Modify a Data Access Page

Menu Method

- [ ] Create a new data access page in Page Design View
- [ ] If a message box appears regarding Access 2000, click **OK**
- [ ] Click **View** on the menu bar, then click **Field List** to display the Field List task pane if necessary
- [ ] Click the **Expand button** ➕ to the left of the table to view all of the fields of that table in the Field List
- [ ] Individually drag each field from the table in the Field List to the Drag fields from the Field List and drop them on the page section of the page
- [ ] Click the **Click here and type title text** placeholder, then type the title

Button Method

- [ ] Create a new data access page in Page Design View
- [ ] If a message box appears regarding Access 2000, click **OK**
- [ ] Click the **Field List button** ▦ on the Page Design toolbar to display the Field List task pane if necessary
- [ ] Follow the steps in the fourth through sixth bullets in the Create and Modify a Data Access Page Menu Method above

Save PivotTable and PivotChart Views to Data Access Pages

Create a PivotTable on a Data Access Page

Menu Method

- [ ] Create a new data access page in Page Design View
- [ ] If a message box appears regarding Access 2000, click **OK**
- [ ] Click **View** on the menu bar, then click **Field List** to open the Field List task pane if necessary
- [ ] In the Field List task pane, click the **Expand button** ➕ to the left of the Queries folder to view all of the queries
- [ ] Individually drag the appropriate query to the Drag fields from the Field List and drop them on the page section of the page
- [ ] In the Layout Wizard dialog box, click the **PivotTable option button**, then click **OK**

Button Method

- [ ] Create a new data access page in Page Design View
- [ ] If a message box appears regarding Access 2000, click **OK**
- [ ] Click the **Field List button** ▦ on the Page Design toolbar to display the Field List task pane if necessary
- [ ] Follow the fourth through sixth bullets in the Create a PivotTable on a Data Access Page Menu Method above

Create a PivotChart on a Data Access Page

Menu Method

- ☐ Create a new data access page in Page Design View
- ☐ If a message box appears regarding Access 2000, click **OK**
- ☐ Click **View** on the menu bar, then click **Field List** to display the Field List task pane if necessary
- ☐ In the Field List task pane, click the **Expand button** + to the left of the Queries folder to view all of the queries, then drag the query to the Drag fields from the Field List and drop them on the page section of the page
- ☐ In the Layout Wizard dialog box, click **PivotChart**, then click **OK**
- ☐ Drag the fields from Tables or Queries as indicated on the Pivot Chart to create the chart

Button Method

- ☐ Create a new data access page in Page Design View
- ☐ If a message box appears regarding Access 2000, click **OK**
- ☐ Click the **Field List button** 🔲 on the Page Design toolbar to display the Field List task pane if necessary
- ☐ Follow the fourth through sixth bullets in the Create a PivotChart on a Data Access Page Menu Method above

ACCESS SKILL SET 15: USING ACCESS TOOLS

IMPORT XML DOCUMENTS INTO ACCESS

Menu Method

- ☐ Click **File** on the menu bar, point to **Get External Data**, then click **Import**
- ☐ In the Import dialog box, click the **Look in list arrow**, then navigate to the appropriate drive and folder
- ☐ Click the **Files of type list arrow**, click **XML Documents**, click the file, then click **Import**
- ☐ In the **Import XML** dialog box, click **OK**
- ☐ Click **OK** when prompted that the import process was finished

EXPORT ACCESS DATA TO XML DOCUMENTS

Menu Method

- ☐ Click the **Tables button** ▦ Tables on the Objects bar if necessary, then click the table
- ☐ Click **File** on the menu bar, then click **Export**
- ☐ In the Export To dialog box, click the **Save in list arrow**, navigate to the appropriate drive and folder, click the **Save as type list arrow**, click **XML Documents**, type the filename, then click **Export**
- ☐ In the Export XML dialog box, click the appropriate check boxes, then click **OK**

ENCRYPT AND DECRYPT DATABASES

Encrypt Databases

Menu Method

- ☐ Close all open databases
- ☐ Click **Tools** on the menu bar, point to **Security**, then click **Encrypt/Decrypt Database**
- ☐ In the Encrypt/Decrypt Database dialog box, click the **Look in list arrow**, navigate to the appropriate drive and folder, click the database name, then click **OK**
- ☐ In the Encrypt Database As dialog box, type the name of the encrypted file in the Filename text box, then click **Save**

Decrypt Databases

Menu Method

- ☐ Close all open databases
- ☐ Click **Tools** on the menu bar, point to **Security**, then click **Encrypt/Decrypt Database**
- ☐ In the Encrypt/Decrypt Database dialog box, click the **Look in list arrow**, navigate to the appropriate drive and folder, click the encrypted database name, then click **OK**
- ☐ In the Decrypt Database As dialog box, type the name to save the decrypted database in the Filename text box, then click **Save**

COMPACT AND REPAIR DATABASES

Menu Method

☐ Close all open databases
☐ Click **Tools** on the menu bar, point to **Database Utilities**, then click **Compact and Repair Database**
☐ In the Database to Compact From dialog box, click the **Look in list arrow**, navigate to the appropriate drive and folder, click the database, then click **Compact**
☐ In the Compact Database Into dialog box, click the **Save in list arrow**, navigate to the appropriate drive and folder, type the filename, then click **Save**

ASSIGN DATABASE SECURITY

Set a Database Password

Menu Method

☐ Close all open databases, click **File** on the menu bar, then click **Open**
☐ In the Open dialog box, navigate to the appropriate drive and folder, then click the filename
☐ Click the **Open list arrow**, then click **Open Exclusive**
☐ Click **Tools** on the menu bar, point to **Security**, then click **Set Database Password**
☐ In the Set Database Password dialog box, enter and verify the password, then click **OK**

Create Workgroups

Menu Method

☐ Close all open databases
☐ Click **Tools** on the menu bar, point to **Security**, then click **Workgroup Administrator**
☐ Click **Create** in the Workgroup Administrator dialog box, type **your initials** in the Workgroup ID text box, then click **OK**
☐ Click **OK** in the Workgroup Information File dialog box, click **OK** in the Confirm Workgroup Information dialog box, then click **OK** in the message box
☐ Click **Join** in the Workgroup Administrator dialog box, click **OK** in the Workgroup Information File dialog box, click **OK** when prompted that you have successfully joined the workgroup, then click **OK** to close the Workgroup Administrator dialog box

Create Permissions

Menu Method

☐ Click **Tools** on the menu bar, point to **Security**, then click **User and Group Permissions**
☐ In the User and Group Permissions dialog box, select the appropriate options using Table AC-17 as a reference, then click **OK**

Table AC-17 Workgroup Permissions

Permission	User can
Open/Run	Open a database, form, or report, or run a macro
Open Exclusive	Open a database with exclusive access
Read Design	View objects in Design View
Modify Design	View, change the design, and delete objects
Administer	For a database: set a password, replicate, or change start properties For all objects: have total access to objects and data, (including ability to assign permissions)
Read Data	View data in tables and queries
Update Data	View and modify records in tables and queries, but not insert or delete records
Insert Data	View and insert data in tables and queries, but not delete or modify
Delete Data	View and delete data in tables and queries, but not insert or modify

Replicate a Database

Menu Method

☐ Click **Tools** on the menu bar, point to **Replication**, then click **Create Replica**
☐ Click **Yes** in the message box to close the database
☐ Click **Yes** in the message box to make a backup of the database and convert the database to a Design Master
☐ In the **Location of New Replica** dialog box, select the location, select any other appropriate options, then click **OK**
☐ Click **OK** in the message box

ACCESS SKILL SET 16: CREATING DATABASE APPLICATIONS

CREATE ACCESS MODULES

Create a Class Module in a Form Using the Command Button Wizard

Menu Method
- ☐ Open the form in Design View
- ☐ Click the **Command Button button** 🔲 on the Toolbox toolbar, then click the form where you want the command to appear
- ☐ Navigate through the Command Button Wizard, making changes or accepting the defaults to create the button as appropriate, then click **Finish**

Create a Global Module to Store a Custom Function

Menu Method
- ☐ Open a new module
- ☐ Create the VBA function
- ☐ Click the **Save button** 🔲 on the Standard Buttons toolbar
- ☐ In the Save As dialog box, type the module name in the Module Name text box, then click **OK**

USE THE DATABASE SPLITTER

Menu Method
- ☐ Click **Tools** on the menu bar, point to **Database Utilities**, then click **Database Splitter**
- ☐ In the Database Splitter dialog box, click **Split Database**
- ☐ In the Create Back-end Database dialog box, click the **Save in list arrow**, navigate to the appropriate drive and folder, then click **Split** to save the back-end database
- ☐ When the message box appears stating the split was successful, click **OK**

Create an MDE File

Menu Method
- ☐ Click **Tools** on the menu bar, point to **Database Utilities**, point to **Convert Database**, then click **To Access 2002 File Format**
- ☐ In the Convert Database Into dialog box, click the **Save in list arrow**, navigate to the appropriate drive and folder, type the filename in the File name text box, click **Save**, then click **OK** when prompted about Access 2000
- ☐ Close all databases, click **Tools** on the menu bar, point to **Database Utilities**, then click **Make MDE File**

☐ In the Database to Save as MDE dialog box, click the **Look in list arrow**, navigate to the appropriate drive and folder, click the database whose format you just changed to 2002, then click **Make MDE**

☐ In the Save MDE As dialog box, type the filename, then click **Save**

MICROSOFT POWERPOINT 2002
EXAM REFERENCE
Getting Started with PowerPoint 2002

The PowerPoint MOUS exam assumes a basic level of proficiency in PowerPoint. This section is intended to help you reference these basic skills while you are preparing to take the PowerPoint Comprehensive exam.

> ☐ Starting and exiting PowerPoint
> ☐ Viewing the Presentation window
> ☐ Using toolbars
> ☐ Using task panes
> ☐ Opening and closing presentations
> ☐ Navigating in the Presentation window
> ☐ Changing views
> ☐ Saving presentations
> ☐ Getting Help

START AND EXIT POWERPOINT

Start PowerPoint

Button Method

☐ Click the **Start button** 🔳**Start** on the Windows taskbar
☐ Point to **Programs or All Programs**
☐ Click **Microsoft PowerPoint**

OR

☐ Double-click the **Microsoft PowerPoint program icon** 🖻 on the desktop

Exit PowerPoint

Menu Method

☐ Click **File** on the menu bar, then click **Exit**

Button Method

☐ Click the **Close button** ☒ on the program window title bar

VIEW THE PRESENTATION WINDOW

Figure PPT-1   PowerPoint Window

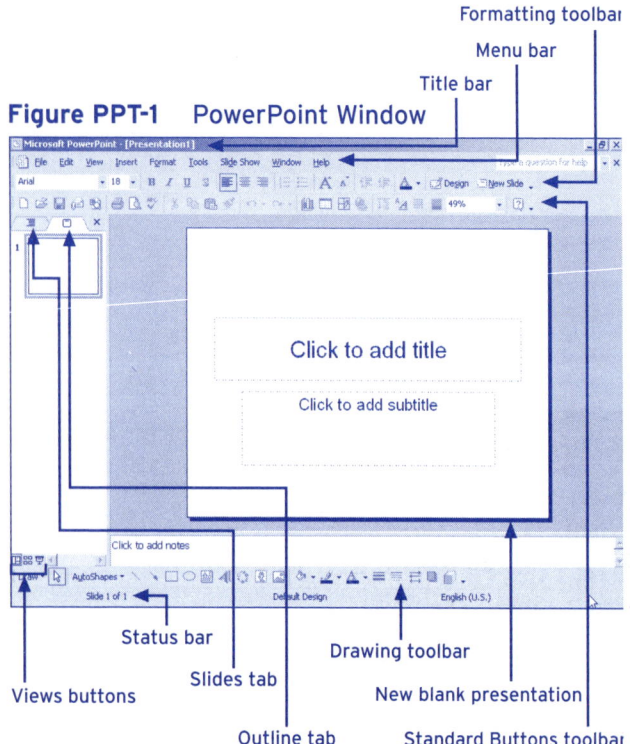

Formatting toolbar

Menu bar

Title bar

Status bar

Views buttons

Slides tab

Outline tab

Drawing toolbar

New blank presentation

Standard Buttons toolbar

USE TOOLBARS

Display Toolbars

Menu Method

☐ Click **View** on the menu bar, point to **Toolbars**, then click the toolbar to display

OR

☐ Right-click any toolbar, then click the toolbar to display on the shortcut menu

Customize Toolbars

Menu Method

☐ Click **Tools** on the menu bar, then click **Customize**, or right-click any toolbar, then click **Customize** on the shortcut menu
☐ In the Customize dialog box, select the appropriate options
☐ Click **Close** in the Customize dialog box

OR

☐ Click **View** on the menu bar, point to **Toolbars**, then click **Customize**
☐ In the Customize dialog box, select the appropriate options
☐ Click **Close** in the Customize dialog box

Button Method

☐ Click the **Toolbar Options button** 🎦 to the right of the toolbar to customize
☐ Point to **Add or Remove Buttons**, then click **Customize**
☐ Follow the steps in the second and third bullets in the Customize Toolbars Menu Method above

Reposition Toolbars

Mouse Method

☐ To move a toolbar, position the pointer over any blank area of the toolbar (not over a button)
☐ When the pointer changes to ✛, press and hold the mouse button
☐ Drag the toolbar to a different location, then release the mouse button

USE TASK PANES

Menu Method

☐ If the task pane is not open, click **View** on the menu bar, point to **Toolbars**, then click **Task Pane**, or right click the **Standard Buttons toolbar**, then click **Task Pane** on the shortcut menu
☐ Click the **Other Task Panes list arrow** ▼ on the task pane title bar, then click the appropriate task pane
☐ Click the **Back button** ◈ or the **Next button** ◈ on the task pane title bar to navigate to previously displayed task panes
☐ Click the **Close button** ✕ on the task pane title bar to close the task pane

OPEN AND CLOSE PRESENTATIONS

Open an Existing Presentation

Menu Method

☐ Click **File** on the menu bar, then click **Open**
☐ In the Open dialog box, navigate to the appropriate drive and folder
☐ Click the file, then click **Open**

Task Pane Method

☐ Click a presentation under the Open a presentation section of the New Presentation task pane or click **More presentations** under the Open a presentation section

☐ Follow the second and third bullets in the Open an Existing Presentation Menu Method above

Button Method

☐ Click the **Open button** 🖼 on the Standard Buttons toolbar

☐ Follow the second and third bullets in the Open an Existing Presentation Menu Method above

Keyboard Method

☐ Press **[Ctrl][O]**

☐ Follow the second and third bullets in the Open an Existing Presentation Menu Method above

Close Presentations

Menu Method

☐ Click **File** on the menu bar, then click **Close**

☐ If prompted to save the presentation, click **Yes** or **No** as appropriate

Button Method

☐ Click the **Close Window button** ☒ on the menu bar

☐ If prompted to save the presentation, click **Yes** or **No** as appropriate

Keyboard Method

☐ Press **[Ctrl][W]**

☐ If prompted to save the presentation, click **Yes** or **No** as appropriate

---

NAVIGATE IN THE PRESENTATION WINDOW

Table PPT 1: Keyboard Navigation Techniques

Key	Moves the insertion point
[Ctrl][Home] or [Ctrl][End]	To the beginning or end of the currently selected text box, or to the first or last slide on the Outline tab (if no slide object is selected)
[Home] or [End]	To the beginning or end of the line of text in a selected text box
[Page Down], [Page Up]	Down or up one slide at a time
[Tab] or [Shift][Tab]	Between objects on a slide

CHANGE VIEWS

Menu Method

☐ Click **View** on the menu bar, then click the view you want using Table PPT-2 as a reference

Button Method

☐ Click the appropriate View button using Table PPT-2 as a reference

Table PPT-2: PowerPoint Views

Button	View	Description
🔲	Normal view	Consists of four work areas: **Outline tab** (used to edit slide text) **Slides tab** (used to navigate) **Slide tab** (used to edit text and graphics) **Notes pane** (used to enter speaker notes)
🔳	Slide Sorter view	Used to rearrange slide order and create animation and transition effects and to see every slide in the presentation at once
🖥	Slide Show view	Each slide fills the screen and you navigate through the presentation as you would when you deliver the presentation.

SAVE PRESENTATIONS

Menu Method

☐ Click **File** on the menu bar, then click **Save**

Button Method

☐ Click the **Save button** 🖫 on the Standard Buttons toolbar

Keyboard Method

☐ Press **[Ctrl][S]**

GET HELP

Menu Method

☐ Click **Help** on the menu bar, then click **Microsoft PowerPoint Help**
☐ Use Table PPT-3 as a reference to select the most appropriate way to search for help using the Microsoft PowerPoint Help window

Button Method

☐ Click the **Microsoft PowerPoint Help button** 🗗 on the Standard Buttons toolbar

☐ Use Table PPT-3 as a reference to select the most appropriate way to search for help using the Microsoft PowerPoint Help window

OR

☐ Click the **Ask a Question box** [Type a question for help ▾] on the menu bar

☐ Type your question, then press **[Enter]**

☐ Select the option you want from the drop-down list, then read about your question in the Microsoft PowerPoint Help window, using Table PPT-3 as a reference

Keyboard Method

☐ Press **[F1]**

☐ Use Table PPT-3 as a reference to select the most appropriate way to search for help using the Microsoft PowerPoint Help window

Table PPT-3: Microsoft Help Window Tabs

Tab	To use:
Contents	Click the **Expand indicator** ⊞ next to each topic you want to explore further, then click the selection you want and read the results in the right pane
Answer Wizard	Type your question in the What would you like to do? text box, click **Search**, then read the results in the right pane
Index	Type the keyword(s) you want to search for in the Type keywords text box, click **Search**, then read the results in the right pane

PowerPoint COMPREHENSIVE Exam
Reference

Skill Sets:

1 Creating presentations
2 Inserting and Modifying Text
3 Inserting and Modifying Visual Elements
4 Modifying Presentation Formats
5 Printing Presentations
6 Working with Data from Other Sources
7 Managing and Delivering Presentations
8 Workgroup Collaboration

PowerPoint Skill Set 1: Creating Presentations

Create Presentations Manually and Use Automated Tools

Create Presentations from a Blank Presentation

Menu Method

☐ Click **File** on the menu bar, then click **New**
☐ In the New Presentation task pane, click **Blank Presentation** under the New section
☐ Type the text you want to appear on the first slide, using text placeholders as appropriate
☐ Click **Insert** on the menu bar, then click **New Slide**

Button Method

☐ Click the **New button** ▢ on the Standard Buttons toolbar
☐ Type the text you want to appear on the first slide, using text placeholders as appropriate
☐ Click the **New Slide button** ▢ on the Formatting toolbar

Keyboard Method

☐ Press **[Ctrl][N]**
☐ Type the text you want to appear on the first slide, using text placeholders as appropriate
☐ Press **[Ctrl][M]** to add a new slide

Create Presentations Using the AutoContent Wizard

Menu Method

☐ Click **File** on the menu bar, then click **New**
☐ Click **From AutoContent Wizard** under the New section in the New Presentation task pane
☐ Navigate through the AutoContent Wizard, making changes or accepting the defaults as appropriate to create the presentation, then click **Finish**

Create Presentations Using Design Templates

Menu Method

☐ Click **File** on the menu bar, then click **New**

☐ Click **From Design Template** under the New section in the New Presentation task pane

☐ In the Slide Design task pane, click the appropriate template in the Apply a design template section

ADD SLIDES TO AND DELETE SLIDES FROM PRESENTATIONS

Add Slides to Presentations

Menu Method

☐ On the Slides or Outline tab, click the slide that is to appear before the new slide

☐ Click **Insert** on the menu bar, then click **New Slide**, or right-click, then click **New Slide** on the shortcut menu

Button Method

☐ On the Slides or Outline tab, click the slide that is to appear before the new slide

☐ Click the **New Slide button** 🔲 on the Formatting toolbar

Keyboard Method

☐ On the Slides or Outline tab, click the slide that is to appear before the new slide

☐ Press **[Ctrl][M]**, or press **[Enter]**

DELETE SLIDES FROM PRESENTATIONS

Menu Method

☐ On the Slides or Outline tab, click the appropriate slide

☐ Click **Edit** on the menu bar, then click **Delete Slide**, or right-click, then click **Delete Slide** on the shortcut menu

Keyboard Method

☐ On the Slides or Outline tab, click the appropriate slide

☐ Press **[Delete]**, or press **[Ctrl][X]**

MODIFY HEADERS AND FOOTERS IN THE SLIDE MASTER

Add Information to the Slide Master

Menu Method

- [ ] Click **View** on the menu bar, point to **Master**, then click **Slide Master**
- [ ] Click the appropriate element on the Slide Master and add the appropriate information
- [ ] Click **Close Master View** on the Slide Master View toolbar

Add Information to the Footer area of the Slide Master

Menu Method

- [ ] Click **View** on the menu bar, then click **Header and Footer**
- [ ] In the Header and Footer dialog box, verify that the **Footer check box** is selected
- [ ] Click the **Footer text box**, then add the appropriate information to the footer
- [ ] Click **Apply** or **Apply to All** as appropriate

    OR

- [ ] Click **View** on the menu bar, point to **Master**, then click **Slide Master**
- [ ] Click the **Footer text box**, then add the appropriate information to the footer
- [ ] Click **Close Master View** on the Slide Master View toolbar

Modify Headers and Footers in Handouts and Notes Pages

Menu Method

- [ ] Click **View** on the menu bar, then click **Header and Footer**
- [ ] In the Header and Footer dialog box, click the **Notes and Handouts tab**
- [ ] Verify that the **Header check box** is selected, click the **Header text box**, then make the appropriate changes
- [ ] Verify that the **Footer check box** is selected, click the **Footer text box**, then make the appropriate changes
- [ ] Click **Apply to All**

    OR

- [ ] Click **View** on the menu bar, point to **Master**, then click **Handout Master** or **Notes Master**
- [ ] Click the **Header Area** or **Footer Area text box**, then make the appropriate text changes
- [ ] Click **Close Master View** on the Handout or Notes Master View toolbar

POWERPOINT SKILL SET 2: INSERTING AND MODIFYING TEXT

IMPORT TEXT FROM WORD

Open a Word Outline as a Presentation

Menu Method

- ☐ Click **Insert** on the menu bar, then click **Slides from Outline**
- ☐ In the Insert Outline dialog box, click the **Look in list arrow**, then navigate to the appropriate drive and folder
- ☐ Click the filename for the Word outline, then click **Insert**

INSERT, FORMAT, AND MODIFY TEXT

Add Body or Title Text to Slides

Menu Method

- ☐ On the Slides or Outline tab, select the appropriate slide
- ☐ Click **Click to add text** or **Click to add title**
- ☐ Type the appropriate text

Add Text Boxes to Slides

Menu Method

- ☐ On the Slides or Outline tab, select the appropriate slide
- ☐ Click **Insert** on the menu bar, then click **Text Box**
- ☐ Click the appropriate location on the slide, then type the text

Button Method

- ☐ On the Slides or Outline tab, select the appropriate slide
- ☐ Click the **Text Box button** on the Drawing toolbar
- ☐ Click the appropriate location on the slide, then type the text

Add Text to an AutoShape

Menu Method

- ☐ On the Slides or Outline tab, select the appropriate slide
- ☐ Click **Insert** on the menu bar, point to **Picture**, then click **AutoShapes**
- ☐ Select the appropriate AutoShape from the AutoShapes toolbar using Table PPT-4 as a reference
- ☐ Click the appropriate location on the slide, type the AutoShape text, then resize the AutoShape to fit the text if necessary

Button Method

☐ On the Slides or Outline tab, select the appropriate slide
☐ Click the **AutoShapes list arrow** on the Drawing toolbar, then select the appropriate AutoShape from the pallette, using Table PPT-4 as a reference
☐ Click the appropriate location on the slide, type the AutoShape text, then resize the AutoShape to fit the text if necessary

Table PPT-4: AutoShape Toolbar and Palette Buttons

Button	Allows you to select a variety of:
	Lines
	Connectors
	Basic Shapes
	Block Arrows
	Flowcharts
	Stars and Banners
	Callouts
	Action Buttons
	More AutoShapes

Add WordArt

Menu Method

☐ On the Slides or Outline tab, select the appropriate slide
☐ Click **Insert** on the menu bar, point to **Picture**, then click **WordArt**
☐ In the WordArt Gallery, click the appropriate style, then click **OK**
☐ In the Edit WordArt Text dialog box, type the text, format the WordArt text as appropriate, then click **OK**
☐ Use ✛ to drag the WordArt object to the appropriate location on the slide

Button Method

☐ On the Slides or Outline tab, select the appropriate slide
☐ Click the **Insert WordArt button** 🖺 on the Drawing toolbar
☐ Follow the third through fifth bullets in the Add WordArt Menu Method above

Edit Text on Slides

Keyboard Method

☐ On the Slides or Outline tab, select the appropriate slide
☐ Select the text on the slide
☐ Edit the text appropriately, using Table PPT-5 as a reference

Table PPT-5: Keyboard Editing Techniques

Effect	Keyboard
Deletes one character to the left	[Backspace]
Deletes one word to the left	[Ctrl][Backspace]
Deletes one word to the right	[Ctrl][Delete]
Deletes one character to the right	[Delete]

Format Text on Slides

Menu Method

☐ On the Slides or Outline tab, select the appropriate slide
☐ Select the text to format
☐ Click **Format** on the menu bar, then click **Font**
☐ In the Font dialog box, make the appropriate selections, then click **OK**

Button Method

☐ On the Slides or Outline tab, select the appropriate slide
☐ Select the text to format
☐ Format the text by clicking the appropriate button on the Formatting toolbar, using Table PPT-6 as a reference

Keyboard Method

☐ On the Slides or Outline tab, select the appropriate slide
☐ Select the text to format
☐ Format the text by pressing the appropriate keyboard combination, using Table PPT-6 as a reference

Table PPT-6: Formatting Effects

Formatting effect	Button	Keyboard
Change the font color		
Change the font type	Times New Roman	[Ctrl][T]
Increase font size		[Ctrl][]] (right bracket)
Decrease font size		[Ctrl][[] (left bracket)
Bold face	B	[Ctrl][B]
Italic	I	[Ctrl][I]
Underline	U	[Ctrl][U]
Shadow	S	
Left align		[Ctrl][L]
Center align		[Ctrl][E]
Right align		[Ctrl][R]
Justify		[Ctrl][J]

PowerPoint Skill Set 3: Inserting and Modifying Visual Elements

Add Tables, Charts, Clip Art, and Bitmap Images to Slides

Create Tables on Slides

Menu Method

☐ On the Slides or Outline tab, select the appropriate slide
☐ Click **Insert** on the menu bar, then click **Table**
☐ In the Insert Table dialog box, select the number of rows and columns, then click **OK**
☐ Type the text in the table, using Table PPT-7 as a reference to navigate between cells

Button Method

☐ On the Slides or Outline tab, select the appropriate slide
☐ Click the **Insert Table button** 🔲 on the Standard Buttons toolbar
☐ On the pallette, drag to select the number of columns and rows, then click the **left mouse button**
☐ Type the text in the table, using Table PPT-7 as a reference to navigate between cells

   OR

☐ On the Slides or Outline tab, select the appropriate slide
☐ Click the **Draw Table button** 🔲 on the Tables and Borders toolbar
☐ Draw columns and rows using ✏
☐ Type the text in the table, using Table PPT-7 as a reference to navigate between cells

Task Pane Method

☐ On the Slides or Outline tab, select the appropriate slide
☐ Click the appropriate Content Layout option in the Content Layouts section of the Slide Layout task pane (Note: Do not use the Blank layout option)
☐ Click the **Insert Table button** 🔲 on the content layout placeholder
☐ Follow the third and fourth bullets in the Create Tables on Slides Menu Method above

Table PPT-7: Table Navigation Techniques

Keyboard	Effect
[Tab]	Moves to the next cell; at the end of a table, inserts a new row
[Shift][Tab]	Moves to the preceding cell
↓	Moves to the next row
↑	Moves to the preceding row

Add Clip Art Images to Slides

Menu Method

- □ On the Slides or Outline tab, select the appropriate slide
- □ Click **Insert** on the menu bar, point to **Picture**, then click **Clip Art**
- □ In the Insert Clip Art task pane, type the search criterion in the Search text text box, then click **Search**
- □ Select a clip art image from the search results
- □ Position the pointer over the image until a list arrow appears, click the **list arrow**, then click **Insert**
- □ Use ✛ to place the image appropriately on the slide

Button Method

- □ On the Slides or Outline tab, select the appropriate slide
- □ Click the **Insert Clip Art button** 🔲 on the Drawing toolbar
- □ Follow the third through sixth bullets in the Add Clip Art Images to Slides Menu Method above

Task Pane Method

- □ On the Slides or Outline tab, select the appropriate slide
- □ Click the appropriate Content Layout option in the Content Layouts section of the Slide Layout task pane (Note: Do not use the Blank layout option)
- □ Click the **Insert Clip Art button** 🔲 on the content layout placeholder
- □ In the Select Picture dialog box, type the search criterion in the Search text text box, then click **Search**
- □ Select the appropriate image from the search results, then click **OK**
- □ Use ✛ to place the image appropriately on the slide

Add Charts to Slides

Menu Method

- □ On the Slides or Outline tab, select the appropriate slide
- □ Click **Insert** on the menu bar, then click **Chart**
- □ Type the data for the chart in the Datasheet, pressing **[Tab]** to navigate between cells
- □ Click the **Datasheet Close button** to close the datasheet

Button Method

- □ On the Slides or Outline tab, select the appropriate slide
- □ Click the **Insert Chart button** 🔲 on the Standard Buttons toolbar
- □ Follow the second through fourth bullets in the Add Charts to Slides Menu Method above

Task Pane Method

- □ On the Slides or Outline tab, select the appropriate slide
- □ Click the appropriate Content Layout option in the Content Layouts section of the Slide Layout task pane (Note: Do not use the Blank layout option)
- □ Click the **Insert Chart button** 🔲 on the content layout placeholder
- □ Follow the second through fourth bullets in the Add Charts to Slides Menu Method above

Add Bitmap Images to Slides

Menu Method

- [ ] On the Slides or Outline tab, select the appropriate slide
- [ ] Click **Insert** on the menu bar, point to **Picture**, then click **From File**
- [ ] In the Insert Picture dialog box, navigate to the appropriate drive and folder
- [ ] Click the appropriate image, then click **Insert**

Button Method

- [ ] On the Slides or Outline tab, select the appropriate slide
- [ ] Click the **Insert Picture button** 🖼 on the Drawing toolbar
- [ ] Follow the third and fourth bullets in the Add Bitmap Images to Slides Menu Method above

Task Pane Method

- [ ] On the Slides or Outline tab, select the appropriate slide
- [ ] Click the appropriate Content Layout option in the Content Layouts section of the Slide Layout task pane (Note: Do not use the Blank layout option)
- [ ] Click the **Insert Picture button** 🖼 on the content layout placeholder
- [ ] Follow the third and fourth bullets in the Add Bitmap Images to Slides Menu Method above

---

CUSTOMIZE SLIDE BACKGROUNDS

Add Fill Effects to Slide Backgrounds

Menu Method

- [ ] On the Slides or Outline tab, select the appropriate slide
- [ ] Click **Format** on the menu bar, then click **Background**
- [ ] In the Background dialog box, click the **Background fill list arrow**, then click **Fill Effects**
- [ ] In the Fill Effects dialog box, click the appropriate options, then click **OK**
- [ ] In the Background dialog box, click **Apply** or **Apply to all** as appropriate

Add Bitmap Graphics to Slide Backgrounds

Menu Method

- [ ] On the Slides or Outline tab, select the appropriate slide
- [ ] Click **Format** on the menu bar, then click **Background**
- [ ] In the Background dialog box, click the **Background fill list arrow**, then click **Fill Effects**
- [ ] In the Fill Effects dialog box, click the **Picture tab**, then click **Select Picture**
- [ ] In the Select Picture dialog box, navigate to the appropriate drive and folder, click the image you want, then click **Insert**
- [ ] In the Fill Effects dialog box, click **OK**
- [ ] In the Background dialog box, click **Apply** or **Apply to all** as appropriate

ADD OFFICEART ELEMENTS TO SLIDES

Add Freeform Objects to Slides

Button Method

☐ On the Slides or Outline tab, select the appropriate slide
☐ Click the appropriate button on the Drawing toolbar, using Table PPT-8 as a reference
☐ Position $+$ where you want the upper-left portion of the shape to appear, then drag to create the shape

Table PPT-8: Drawing Toolbar Buttons

Button	Description
Line button	Draws a straight line
Arrow button	Draws an arrow
Oval button	Draws an oval, or a circle when pressing and holding [Shift] while dragging
Rectangle button	Draws a rectangle, or a square when pressing and holding [Shift] while dragging

Add AutoShapes to Slides

☐ To insert an AutoShape, see the activity "Add Text to an AutoShape" in Skill Set 2: Inserting and Modifying Text
☐ To insert WordArt, see the activity "Add WordArt" in Skill Set 2: Inserting and Modifying Text

Add an Organization Chart to a Slide

Menu Method

☐ On the Slides or Outline tab, select the appropriate slide
☐ Click **Insert** on the menu bar, then click **Diagram**
☐ In the Diagram Gallery, click the **Organization Chart option** , then click **OK**

Button Method

☐ On the Slides or Outline tab, select the appropriate slide
☐ Click the **Insert Diagram or Organization Chart button** on the Drawing toolbar
☐ In the Diagram Gallery, click the **Organization Chart option** , then click **OK**

APPLY CUSTOM FORMATS TO TABLES

Apply User-Defined Formats to Tables

Menu Method

- ☐ On the Slides or Outline tab, select the appropriate slide
- ☐ Select the table
- ☐ Click **Format** on the menu bar, then click **Table**
- ☐ In the Format Table dialog box, make the appropriate selections, then click **OK**

Button Method

- ☐ On the Slides or Outline tab, select the appropriate slide
- ☐ Select the table
- ☐ Use the buttons on the Tables and Borders toolbar to make the formatting changes, using Table PPT-9 as a reference

Table PPT-9: Tables and Borders Toolbar Formatting Buttons

Button	Used to
Border Style button	Apply dashed or solid lines as a border
Border Width button	Change the point size of the border
Border Color button	Change the color of the cell or table borders
Borders button	Apply a border around cells or around the table
Fill Color list arrow	Add shading and patterns to selected cells

POWERPOINT SKILL SET 4: MODIFYING PRESENTATION FORMATS

APPLY FORMATS TO PRESENTATIONS

Format Slides Differently in a Single Presentation

Menu Method

□ On the Slides or Outline tab, select the appropriate slide(s)
□ Click **Format** on the menu bar, then click **Slide Design**
□ In the Slide Design task pane, scroll the list of formats, click the **list arrow** for the appropriate format, then click **Apply to Selected Slides**

Button Method

□ On the Slides or Outline tab, select the appropriate slide(s)
□ Click the **Slide Design button** ☑ Design on the Formatting toolbar
□ In the Slide Design task pane, scroll the list of formats, click the **list arrow** for the appropriate format, then click **Apply to Selected Slides**

Modify Presentation Templates

Menu Method

□ Click **View** on the menu bar, point to **Master**, then click **Slide Master**
□ Make the appropriate modifications, using Tables PPT-6 and PPT-10 as references
□ Click **Close Master View** on the Slide Master toolbar

Table PPT-10: Outlining Toolbar Buttons

Button	Used to
⬅	Promote to a more prominent text style
➡	Demote to a less prominent text style
⬆	Move up a line in the text box
⬇	Move down a line in the text box

Modify the Format of Individual Slides

Button Method

□ On the Slides or Outline tab, select the appropriate slide(s)
□ Make the modifications using Table PPT-6 as a reference

Apply More than One Design Template to Presentations

Button Method

□ On the Slides or Outline tab, select the appropriate slide(s)
□ Click the **Slide Design button** ☑ Design on the Formatting toolbar
□ In the Slide Design task pane, click **Design Templates**
□ Scroll the list of templates, click the **list arrow** for the template you want, then click **Apply to Selected Slides**

☐ Repeat the first through fourth bullets to apply other templates to other slides

APPLY ANIMATION SCHEMES

Apply an Animation Scheme to a Single Slide

Menu Method

☐ On the Slides or Outline tab, select the appropriate slide
☐ Click **Slide Show** on the menu bar, then click **Animation Schemes**
☐ In the Slide Design task pane, click the appropriate scheme

Button Method

☐ On the Slides or Outline tab, select the appropriate slide
☐ Click the **Slide Design button** `Design` on the Formatting toolbar
☐ In the Slide Design task pane, click **Animation Schemes**
☐ In the Slide Design task pane, click the appropriate scheme

Apply an Animation Scheme to a Group of Slides

Menu Method

☐ On the Slides or Outline tab, select the appropriate slides
☐ Click **Slide Show** on the menu bar, then click **Animation Schemes**
☐ In the Slide Design task pane, click the appropriate scheme

Button Method

☐ On the Slides or Outline tab, select the appropriate slides
☐ Click the **Slide Design button** on the Formatting toolbar
☐ In the Slide Design task pane, click **Animation Schemes**
☐ In the Slide Design task pane, click the appropriate scheme

Apply an Animation Scheme to an Entire Presentation

Menu Method

☐ Click **Slide Show** on the menu bar, then click **Animation Schemes**
☐ In the Slide Design task pane, click the appropriate scheme
☐ In the Slide Design task pane, click **Apply to All Slides**

Button Method

☐ Click the **Slide Design button** `Design` on the Formatting toolbar
☐ In the Slide Design task pane, click **Animation Schemes**
☐ Follow the second and third bullets in the Apply an Animation Scheme to an Entire Presentation Menu Method above

APPLY SLIDE TRANSITIONS

Apply Transition Effects to a Single Slide

Menu Method
☐ On the Slides or Outline tab, select the appropriate slide
☐ Click **Slide Show** on the menu bar, then click **Slide Transition**
☐ In the Slide Transition task pane, scroll the list of transitions, then select the appropriate options

Apply Transition Effects to a Group of Slides in a Presentation

Menu Method
☐ On the Slides or Outline tab, select the appropriate slides
☐ Click **Slide Show** on the menu bar, then click **Slide Transition**
☐ In the Slide Transition task pane, scroll the list of transitions, then select the appropriate options

Apply Transition Effects to an Entire Presentation

Menu Method
☐ Click **Slide Show** on the menu bar, then click **Slide Transition**
☐ In the Slide Transition task pane, select the appropriate options
☐ In the Slide Transition task pane, click **Apply to All Slides**

CUSTOMIZE SLIDE FORMATS

Customize Slides
☐ On the Slides or Outline tab, select the appropriate slide
☐ Select the element you want to modify
☐ Use Table PPT-11 to reference examples of types and methods of customization modifications

Table PPT-11: Slide Customization Options

Element	Types of modifications	Menu method	Button method
Title or Body text	Change the font color, resize the font, or add effects such as bold, italics, or underlining	Click **Format** on the menu bar, then click **Font**	Use Table PPT-6 as a reference
Graphics	Add a graphic, such as a chart, picture, clip art, and more	Click **Insert** on the menu bar, then click the appropriate element	Click the appropriate button on the Drawing toolbar using Table PPT-8 as a reference
Background	Add color or texture to the slide background	Click **Format** on the menu bar, then click **Background**	
Animations	Add transition effects to slides such as fading, spiraling, and more	Click **Slide Show** on the menu bar, then click **Animation Schemes**	

CUSTOMIZE SLIDE TEMPLATES

Customize Templates

Menu Method
- [ ] Click **View** on the menu bar, point to **Master**, then click **Slide Master**
- [ ] Click the appropriate slide element
- [ ] Make the appropriate formatting modifications, using Tables PPT-6 and PPT-10 as references
- [ ] Click **File** on the menu bar, then click **Save As**
- [ ] In the Save As dialog box, click the **Save as type list arrow**, then click **Design Template**
- [ ] Type the filename in the File name text box, then click **OK**

MANAGE A SLIDE MASTER

Create and Manage a Slide Master

Menu Method

- [ ] Click **View** on the menu bar, point to **Master**, then click **Slide Master**
- [ ] Click the **Insert New Slide Master button** 🔲 on the Slide Master View toolbar
- [ ] Make the appropriate formatting modifications using Tables PPT-6 and PPT-10 as references
- [ ] Click the **Rename Master button** 🔲 on the Slide Master View toolbar
- [ ] In the Rename Master dialog box, enter a name for the new master, then click **Rename**
- [ ] Click **Close Master View** on the Slide Master View toolbar

Create and Manage Multiple Slide Masters

Menu Method

- [ ] Click **View** on the menu bar, point to **Master**, then click **Slide Master**
- [ ] Click the **Insert New Slide Master button** 🔲 on the Slide Master View toolbar
- [ ] Make the appropriate formatting modifications, using Tables PPT-6 and PPT-10 as references
- [ ] Click the **Rename Master button** 🔲 on the Slide Master View toolbar
- [ ] In the Rename Master dialog box, enter a name for the new master, then click **Rename**
- [ ] Click **Close Master View** on the Slide Master View toolbar
- [ ] On the Slides or Outline tab, select the slides to which you want to apply the new slide master
- [ ] Position the pointer over the new slide master in the Slide Design task pane, click the **list arrow**, then click **Apply to Selected Slides**

Rehearse Timings

Menu Method

- [ ] Click **Slide Show** on the menu bar, then click **Rehearse Timings**
- [ ] Advance through the presentation, clicking the **Next button** 🔲 when finished rehearsing each slide
- [ ] When a message box appears, click **Yes** to keep the new slide timings

REARRANGE SLIDES

Button Method

☐ In the Outlines tab, click the **Move Up button** ⬆ or the **Move Down button** ⬇ on the Outline toolbar

Mouse Method

☐ Click the slide in Slide Sorter view, then drag it to the new location using 🕭

OR

☐ Click the slide on the Slides tab, then drag it to the new location using 🕭

MODIFY SLIDE LAYOUT

Menu Method

☐ On the Slides or Outline tab, select the appropriate slide(s)
☐ Click **Format** on the menu bar, then click **Slide Layout**
☐ Click the appropriate option in the Slide Layout task pane

ADD LINKS TO A PRESENTATION

Add Hyperlinks to Slides

☐ On the Slides or Outline tab, select the appropriate slide
☐ Select the object or text to which you want to apply the hyperlink
☐ Open the Insert Hyperlink dialog box using Table PPT-12 as a reference
☐ Make the appropriate selections, then click **OK**

Table PPT-12: Methods for Opening the Insert Hyperlink Dialog Box

Menu	Button	Keyboard
Click **Insert** on the menu bar, then click **Hyperlink**	Click the Insert **Hyperlink button** 🕭 on the Standard Buttons toolbar	Press [Ctrl][K]

PowerPoint Skill Set 5: Printing Presentations

Preview and Print Slides, Outlines, Handouts, and Speaker Notes

Preview Slides

Menu Method
☐ Click **File** on the menu bar, then click **Print Preview**

Button Method
☐ Click the **Print Preview button** 🔲 on the Standard Buttons toolbar

Print Slides

Menu Method
☐ Click **File** on the menu bar, then click **Print**
☐ In the Print dialog box, click the appropriate options
☐ Click **OK**

Button Method
☐ Click the **Print button** 🖨 on the Standard Buttons toolbar

Keyboard Method
☐ Press **[Ctrl][P]**
☐ Follow the second and third bullets in the Print Slides Menu Method above

Preview and Print Outlines

Menu Method
☐ Click **File** on the menu bar, then click **Print**
☐ In the Print dialog box, click the **Print what list arrow**, then click **Outline View**
☐ Click **Preview**
☐ Click the **Print button** 🖨 on the Print Preview toolbar, then click **OK** in the Print dialog box

Keyboard Method
☐ Press **[Ctrl][P]**
☐ Follow the second through fourth bullets in the Preview and Print Outlines Menu Method above

Preview and Print Handouts

Menu Method
☐ Click **File** on the menu bar, then click **Print**
☐ In the Print dialog box, click the **Print what list arrow**, then click **Handouts**

☐ Click the **Slides per page list arrow** in the Handouts area then click the appropriate handouts option if necessary
☐ Click **Preview**
☐ In the Print Preview window, click the **Print What list arrow**, then click the appropriate option if necessary
☐ Click the **Print button** 🖨 on the Print Preview toolbar, then click **OK** in the Print dialog box

Keyboard Method

☐ Press **[Ctrl][P]**
☐ Follow the second through sixth bullets in the Preview and Print Handouts Menu Method above

Preview and Print Speaker Notes

Menu Method

☐ Click **File** on the menu bar, then click **Print**
☐ In the Print dialog box, click the **Print what list arrow**, then click **Notes Pages**
☐ Click **Preview**
☐ Click the **Print button** 🖨 on the Print Preview toolbar, then click **OK** in the Print dialog box

Keyboard Method

☐ Press **[Ctrl][P]**
☐ Follow the second through fourth bullets in the Preview and Print Speaker Notes Menu Method above

Print Comments Pages

Menu Method

☐ Click **File** on the menu bar, then click **Print**
☐ In the Print dialog box, click the **Print what list arrow**, click **Slides**, then click the **All option button** in the Print range area
☐ Click the **Include comment pages check box** to select it
☐ Click **OK**

Keyboard Method

☐ Press **[Ctrl][P]**
☐ Follow the second through fourth bullets in the Print Comments Pages Menu Method above

PowerPoint Skill Set 6: Working with Data from Other Sources

Import Excel Charts to Slides

Embed Excel Charts on Slides

Menu Method

- ☐ On the Slides or Outline tab, select the appropriate slide
- ☐ Click **Insert** on the menu bar, then click **Object**
- ☐ In the Insert Object dialog box, click the **Create from file option button**, then click **Browse**
- ☐ In the Browse dialog box, navigate to the appropriate drive and folder, click the file, then click **OK**
- ☐ In the Insert Object dialog box, click **OK**

Link Excel Charts to Slides

Menu Method

- ☐ Start Microsoft Excel, click **File** on the menu bar, then click **Open**
- ☐ In the Open dialog box, navigate to the appropriate drive and folder, click the file, then click **Open**
- ☐ Select the chart in the Excel file
- ☐ Click **Edit** on the menu bar, then click **Copy**
- ☐ Click the **Microsoft PowerPoint button** on the task bar
- ☐ On the Slides or Outline tab, select the appropriate slide
- ☐ Click **Edit** on the menu bar, then click **Paste Special**
- ☐ In the Paste Special dialog box, click **Microsoft Excel Chart Object** in the As: text box, click the **Paste link option button**, then click **OK**

Add Sound and Video to Slides

Add Sound Effects to Slides

Menu Method

- ☐ On the Slides or Outline tab, select the appropriate slide
- ☐ Click **Insert** on the menu bar, point to **Movies and Sounds**, then click **Sound from File**
- ☐ In the Insert Sound dialog box, navigate to the appropriate drive and folder, click the sound file, then click **OK**
- ☐ In the message box, click **Yes** or **No** to specify whether the sound will play automatically
- ☐ Use ⛶ to place the sound icon in the appropriate location on the slide

Add Video Effects to Slides

Menu Method

- ☐ On the Slides or Outline tab, select the appropriate slide
- ☐ Click **Insert** on the menu bar, point to **Movies and Sounds**, then click **Movie from File**

☐ In the Insert Movie dialog box, navigate to the appropriate drive and folder, click the movie file, then click **OK**

☐ In the message box, click **Yes** or **No** to specify whether the movie will play automatically

☐ Use ⌖ to place the movie icon in the appropriate location on the slide

INSERT WORD TABLES ON SLIDES

Embed Word Tables on Slides

Menu Method

☐ On the Slides or Outline tab, select the appropriate slide

☐ Click **Insert** on the menu bar, then click **Object**

☐ In the Insert Object dialog box, click the **Create from file option button**, then click **Browse**

☐ In the Browse dialog box, navigate to the appropriate drive and folder, click the file, then click **OK**

☐ In the Insert Object dialog box, click **OK**

Link Word Tables on Slides

Menu Method

☐ On the Slides or Outline tab, select the appropriate slide

☐ Click **Insert** on the menu bar, then click **Object**

☐ In the Insert Object dialog box, click the **Create from file option button**, then click **Browse**

☐ In the Browse dialog box, navigate to the appropriate drive and folder, click the file, then click **OK**

☐ In the Insert Object dialog box, click the **Link check box**, then click **OK**

EXPORT A PRESENTATION AS AN OUTLINE

Menu Method

☐ Click **File** on the menu bar, then click **Save As**

☐ In the Save As dialog box, click the **Save as type list arrow**, then click **Outline/RTF**

☐ Navigate to the appropriate drive and folder, then type the filename in the File name text box

☐ Click **Save**

POWERPOINT SKILL SET 7: MANAGING AND DELIVERING PRESENTATIONS

SET UP SLIDE SHOWS

Menu Method

☐ Click **Slide Show** on the menu bar, then click **Set Up Show**
☐ Click the appropriate options in the Set Up Show dialog box, using Table PPT-13 as an example
☐ Click **OK**

DELIVER PRESENTATIONS

Prepare Slide Shows for Delivery

Menu Method

☐ Click **Slide Show** on the menu bar, then click **Set Up Show**
☐ Click the appropriate options in the Set Up Show dialog box, using Table PPT-13 as an example
☐ Click **OK**

Table PPT-13: Set Up Show Dialog Box Options

Dialog Box Section	Options
Show type	Choose whether show will be delivered by a speaker, or browsed by an individual or at a kiosk
Show options	Select whether to loop, or show with narration or animation
Performance	Set resolution options and graphics accelerator options
Show slides	Select whether to show all or selected slides
Advance slides	Choose to proceed through slides manually or using timings
Multiple monitors	Set show to run on one or multiple options

Run Slide Shows

Menu Method

☐ Click **Slide Show** on the menu bar, then click **View Show**

Button Method

☐ Click the **first slide** in the presentation
☐ Click the **Slide show (from current slide) button** 🖵 on the Status bar

Keyboard Method

☐ Press **[F5]**

Setup a Custom Show

Menu Method

- ☐ Click **Slide Show** on the menu bar, then click **Custom Shows**
- ☐ In the Customs Shows dialog box, click **New**
- ☐ In the Define Custom Show dialog box, click the **Slide show name text box**, then type the name
- ☐ Select each slide, then click **Add** after each
- ☐ Select a slide order by using the **Move Up** 🔼 and **Move Down** 🔽 **buttons**, then click **OK**
- ☐ Click **Close** in the Define Custom Shows dialog box

Use Onscreen Navigation Tools

Menu Method

- ☐ Start the presentation
- ☐ Right-click the slide, then click the appropriate option from the shortcut menu

Keyboard Method

- ☐ Start the presentation
- ☐ Navigate through the presentation, using Table PPT-14 as a reference

Table PPT-14: Slide Show Navigation Keyboard Shortcuts

Press	Effect
[N]; [Enter]; [PgDn]; →; ↓; or [Spacebar]	Perform the next animation or advance to the next slide
[P]; [PgUp]; ←; ↑; or [Backspace]	Perform the previous animation or return to the previous slide
[*Number*][Enter]	Go to slide number
[Esc]; [Ctrl][Break]; or [-] (hyphen)	End a slide show
[Home], or [1][Enter]	Return to the first slide
[End]	Go to the last slide
[Tab]	Go to the first or next hyperlink on a slide
[Shift][Tab]	Go to the last or previous hyperlink on a slide

Mouse Method

☐ Click the **left mouse button** to perform the next animation or advance to the next slide
☐ Press **both mouse buttons** for two seconds to return to the first slide

MANAGE FILES AND FOLDERS FOR PRESENTATIONS

Menu Method

☐ Click **File** on the menu bar, then click **Save As**
☐ In the Save As dialog box, click the **Create New Folder button**
☐ In the New Folder dialog box, type the folder name in the Name text box, then click **OK**
☐ In the Save As dialog box, type the filename in the File name text box, then click **Save**

WORK WITH EMBEDDED FONTS

Menu Method

☐ Click **Tools** on the menu bar, click **Options**
☐ In the Options dialog box, click the **Save tab**
☐ Click the **Embed TrueType fonts check box**, then click **OK**

PUBLISH PRESENTATIONS TO THE WEB

Menu Method

☐ Click **File** on the menu bar, then click **Save as Web Page**
☐ In the Save As dialog box, navigate to the appropriate drive and folder
☐ Type the filename in the File name text box, then click **Save**

USE PACK AND GO

Menu Method

☐ Select a blank formatted floppy disk or CD-ROM onto which to save your presentation
☐ Click **File** on the menu bar, then click **Pack and Go**
☐ Navigate through the Pack and Go Wizard, making changes or accepting the defaults as appropriate, then click **Finish**

POWERPOINT SKILL SET 8: WORKGROUP COLLABORATION

SET UP A REVIEW CYCLE

Menu Method

☐ Click **File** on the menu bar, point to **Send To**, then click **Routing Recipient**

☐ If the Choose Profile dialog box opens, select your **profile name**, then click **OK**

☐ If a message box opens about accessing e-mail addresses stored in Outlook, click **Yes**

☐ In the Add Routing Slip dialog box, click **Address** to open your e-mail program address book

☐ In the Address Book dialog box, select the names of people to whom you want to send the file, clicking **To** after each name, then click **OK**

☐ In the Add Routing Slip dialog box, verify that the appropriate options are selected, then click **Route**

☐ Click **Yes** to access the e-mail addresses if the message box opens, then click **Send** to send the e-mail

REVIEW PRESENTATION COMMENTS

Menu Method

☐ Open the PowerPoint file into which you want to merge a reviewer's comments

☐ Click **Tools** on the menu bar, then click **Compare and Merge Presentations**

☐ In the Choose Files to Merge with Current Presentation dialog box, click the appropriate PowerPoint file, click **Merge**, then click **Continue** in the message box

☐ Click **View** on the menu bar, then click **Markup** to select it if necessary

☐ Place the pointer over the colored box on the slide to read the comment

☐ Click the appropriate button on the Reviewing toolbar to navigate through the comments, using Table PPT-15 as a reference

Table PPT-15: Reviewing Toolbar Buttons

Button	Effect
�'	Shows or hides comments and editing changes
Reviewers...	Displays comments and editing changes for certain reviewers
🔄	Returns to the previous comment or editing change
🔄	Advances to the next comment or editing change
🖊 ▾	Applies editing changes to the current slide or to the entire presentation
🗋 ▾	Undoes the editing changes to the current slide or to the entire presentation
🗨	Inserts a new comment
🗨	Allows a comment to be edited
✕ ▾	Deletes selected comment
🖼	Shows the Revisions Pane

SCHEDULE AND DELIVER PRESENTATION BROADCASTS

Menu Method

☐ Click **Slide Show** on the menu bar, point to **Online Broadcast**, then click **Schedule a Live Broadcast**

☐ Click **Save** if necessary in the warning box

☐ Type the appropriate information in the Schedule Presentation Broadcast dialog box, then click **Settings**

☐ In the Broadcast Settings dialog box, click the **Presenter tab**, then click **Browse**

☐ In the Choose Directory dialog box, navigate to the appropriate drive and shared folder, then click **Select**

☐ If you were able to specify a shared folder on a network, click **OK** in the Schedule Presentation Broadcast dialog box, then click **Schedule** in the Broadcast dialog box, otherwise, close all open dialog boxes

☐ To broadcast the show at the scheduled time, click **Slide Show** on the menu bar, point to **Online Broadcast**, then click **Start Live broadcast now**

PUBLISH PRESENTATIONS TO THE WEB

Menu Method

☐ Click **File** on the menu bar, then click **Save as Web Page**

☐ In the Save As dialog box, navigate to the appropriate drive and folder, make the appropriate selections, then click **Publish**

☐ In the Publish as Web Page dialog box, click the appropriate options, then click **Publish**

MICROSOFT OUTLOOK 2002
EXAM REFERENCE
Getting Started with Outlook 2002

The Outlook Core MOUS exam assumes a basic level of proficiency in Outlook. This section is intended to help you reference these basic skills while you are preparing to take the Outlook Core MOUS exam.

> ☐ Starting and exiting Outlook
> ☐ Setting up an Outlook profile
> ☐ Outlook Tools
> ☐ Using toolbars
> ☐ Navigating in the Outlook window
> ☐ Getting Help

START AND EXIT OUTLOOK

Start Outlook

Button Method
☐ Click the **Start button** 🏁 Start on the Windows taskbar
☐ Point to **Programs** or **All Programs**
☐ Click **Microsoft Outlook**
☐ If this is the first time you have started Outlook, navigate through the First Time Starting Outlook 2002 Wizard making the appropriate selections, then click **Finish**

OR

☐ Double-click the **Microsoft Outlook program icon** 🖥 on the desktop
☐ If this is the first time you have started Outlook, navigate through the First Time Starting Outlook 2002 Wizard making the appropriate selections, then click **Finish**

Exit Outlook

Menu Method
☐ Click **File** on the menu bar, then click **Exit**

Button Method
☐ Click the **Close button** ☒ on the program window title bar

Refreshing the Inbox

Menu Method
☐ Click **Tools** on the menu bar, point to **Send/Receive**, then click the appropriate option

Button Method

☐ In the Inbox window, click the **Send/Receive button** 🔳 on the Standard toolbar

Keyboard Method

☐ Press **[F9]** to send and receive all messages in Outlook

SET UP AN OUTLOOK PROFILE

Button Method

☐ Click the **Start button** 🔳 Start on the Windows taskbar, point to **Settings** if necessary, then click **Control Panel**
☐ In the Control Panel window, double-click the **Mail icon** 🔵
☐ In the Mail Setup – Outlook dialog box, click **Show Profiles**
☐ In the Mail dialog box, click **Add**
☐ In the New Profile dialog box, type a name for the profile in the Profile name text box, then click **OK**
☐ Follow the steps in the E-mail Accounts Wizard, making changes or accepting the defaults as appropriate to create the profile, then click **Finish**
☐ Click **OK** in the Mail dialog box

OUTLOOK TOOLS

The Inbox Window

From the Inbox window you can send, receive, and read mail, as well as read and respond to any task or meeting requests.

Figure OL-1   The Inbox Window

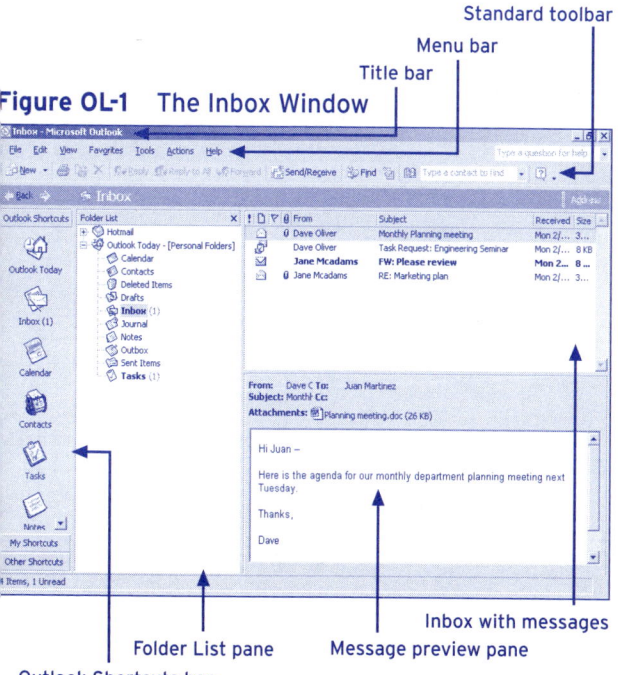

Standard toolbar

Menu bar

Title bar

Inbox with messages

Folder List pane

Message preview pane

Outlook Shortcuts bar

The Calendar Window

You can view the Calendar by a day, week, or month, and you can use the Calendar to create appointments and events, organize meetings, view group schedules, and manage another user's Calendar.

Figure OL-2   The Calendar Window

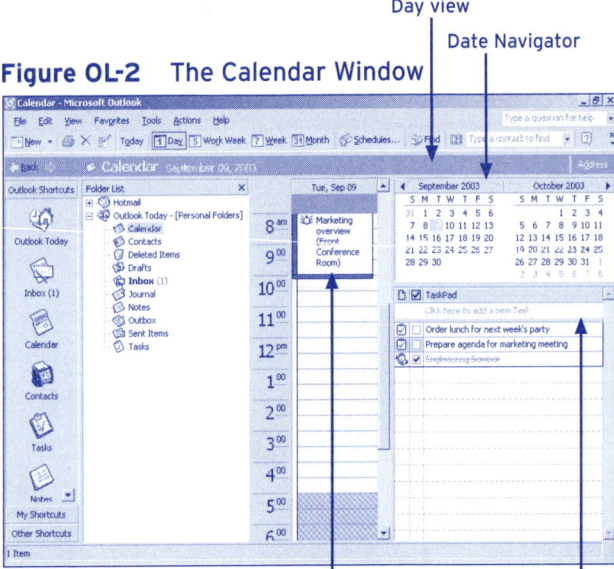

Day view

Date Navigator

Appointment

TaskPad

The Contacts Folder

The Contacts folder is used to store e-mail addresses, addresses, phone numbers, and any other information that relates to your contacts, such as birthdays or spouse's names.

Displays alphabetical
range for currently
displayed contacts

Figure OL-3   The Contacts Folder

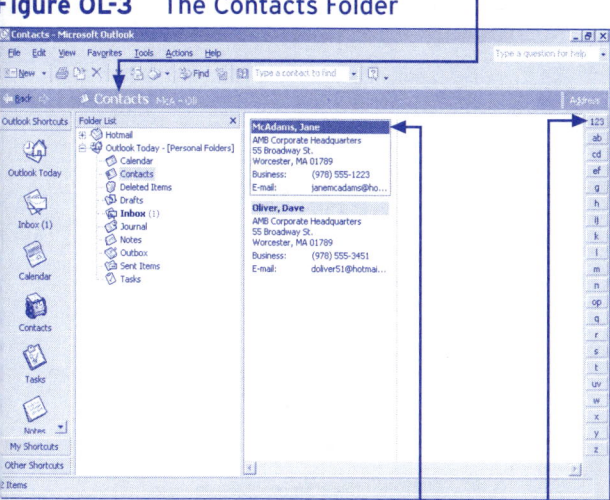

Contact   Contact index

The Tasks Window

The Tasks window contains a list of all tasks you have created for your-self, been assigned, or assigned to others. You can use the list to update the status of your projects, set a task as recurring, delegate tasks, and mark them as completed.

Figure OL-4   The Tasks Window

Selected task

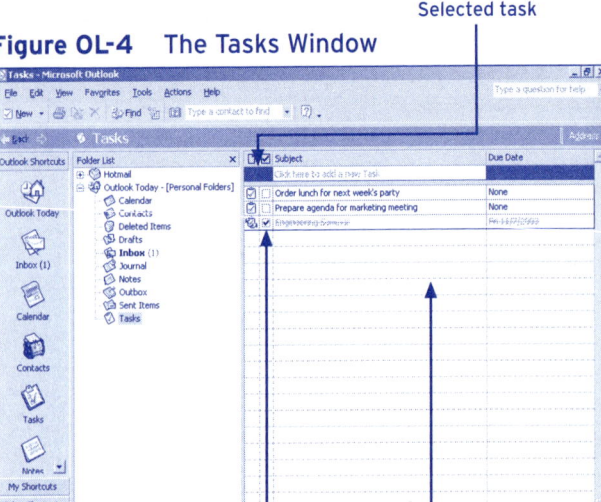

Completed task   TaskPad

The Notes Window

The Notes window is used to keep track of questions, directions, or items you will need in creating a document or when completing a task. You can leave notes open on the screen as you work.

Figure OL-5   The Notes Window

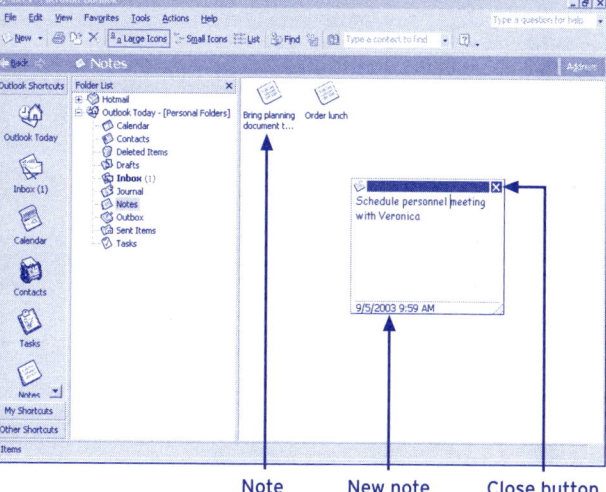

Note   New note   Close button

USE TOOLBARS

Display Toolbars

Menu Method

☐ Click **View** on the menu bar, point to **Toolbars**, then click the toolbar you want to display

OR

☐ Right-click any toolbar, then click the toolbar you want to display on the shortcut menu

Customize Toolbars

Menu Method

☐ Click **Tools** on the menu bar, then click **Customize**, or click **View** on the menu bar, point to **Toolbars**, then click **Customize**, or right-click any toolbar, then click **Customize** on the shortcut menu
☐ In the Customize dialog box, click the **Toolbars tab** if necessary, select the appropriate options, then click **Close**

Button Method

☐ Click the **Toolbar Options button** ⬚ on the toolbar you wish to customize
☐ Point to **Add or Remove Buttons**, then click **Customize**
☐ In the Customize dialog box, click the **Toolbars tab** if necessary, select the appropriate options, then click **Close**

Reposition Toolbars

Mouse Method

☐ Position the pointer over the left edge of the toolbar
☐ When the pointer changes to ✛, press and hold the mouse button
☐ Drag the toolbar to a blank area of the window or to a different location, then release the mouse button

NAVIGATE IN THE OUTLOOK WINDOW

Menu Method

☐ Click **View** on the menu bar, point to **Go To**, then click the appropriate item, using Table OL-1 as a reference

Button Method

☐ Click the **Back button** ⬚ or the **Forward button** ⬚ as appropriate to navigate to previous views
☐ Click the appropriate button on the Outlook Shortcuts bar, using Table OL-1 as a reference

Table OL-1 Selected Outlook Navigation Options

Command on the Go To submenu	Outlook Shortcuts bar button	Description
Folder		Opens the Go to Folder dialog box, from which you can select a view or folder to which to navigate, then click OK
Outlook Today	🏠	Overview of folders' contents and any tasks or appointments for the day
Inbox	📬	View new e-mail messages, create new e-mail messages, and move messages to folders
Drafts		Folder where unsent messages are stored so that you can edit and/or send them later
Calendar	📅	View, create, and manage appointments
Contacts	📇	Create and edit contacts
Tasks	📋	Schedule and assign tasks

Table OL-1 Selected Outlook Navigation Options (continued)

Command on the Go To submenu	Outlook Shortcuts bar button	Description
	🖎	Create and edit notes
	🗑	View and restore deleted items and empty the folder to save disk space

GET HELP

Menu Method

☐ Click **Help** on the menu bar, then click **Microsoft Outlook Help**
☐ Use Table OL-2 as a reference to select the most appropriate way to search for help using the Microsoft Outlook Help window

Button Method

☐ Click the **Microsoft Outlook Help button** 🗹 on the Standard toolbar
☐ Use Table OL-2 as a reference to select the most appropriate way to search for help using the Microsoft Outlook Help window

OR

☐ Click the **Ask a Question box** [Type a question for help ▾] on the menu bar
☐ Type your question, then press **[Enter]**
☐ Select the option you want from the drop down list, then read about your question in the Microsoft Outlook Help window, using Table OL-2 as a reference

Keyboard Method

☐ Press **[F1]**
☐ Use Table OL-2 as a reference to select the most appropriate way to search for help using the Microsoft Outlook Help window

Table OL-2 Microsoft Help Window Tabs

Tab	To use
Contents	Click the Expand indicator ➕ next to each topic you want to explore further, then click the selection you want and read the results in the right pane
Answer Wizard	Type your question in the What would you like to do? text box, click Search, then read the results in the right pane
Index	Type the keyword(s) you want to search for in the Type keywords text box, click Search, then read the results in the right pane

OUTLOOK CORE EXAM REFERENCE

Skill Sets:

1 Creating and viewing messages
2 Scheduling
3 Managing messages
4 Creating and managing contacts
5 Creating and managing Tasks and Notes

OUTLOOK SKILL SET 1: CREATING AND VIEWING MESSAGES

DISPLAY AND PRINT MESSAGES

Open Messages

Menu Method

☐ In the Inbox window, click the appropriate message
☐ Click **File** on the menu bar, point to **Open**, then click **Selected Items**, or right-click the message, then click **Open** on the shortcut menu

Keyboard Method

☐ In the Inbox window, click the appropriate message
☐ Press **[Ctrl][O]**

Mouse Method

☐ In the Inbox window, double-click the appropriate message

Print Messages

Menu Method

☐ In the Inbox window, click the appropriate message to select it, or open the message and maximize the message window
☐ Click **File** on the menu bar, then click **Print**
☐ In the Print dialog box, select the appropriate options, then click **OK**

Button Method

☐ In the Inbox window, click the appropriate message to select it, or open the message and maximize the message window
☐ Click the **Print button** 🖨 on the Standard toolbar

Keyboard Method

☐ In the Inbox window, click the appropriate message to select it, or open the message and maximize the message window
☐ Press **[Ctrl][P]**
☐ In the Print dialog box, select the appropriate options, then click **OK**

COMPOSE AND SEND MESSAGES

Compose and Send Messages

Menu Method

☐ Click **File** on the menu bar, point to **New**, then click **Mail Message**
☐ In the Untitled Message window, type the recipient name(s) or type the e-mail address in the To and Cc boxes, separating each name with a semicolon (;), or to select recipient names from the Address Book, click the **To button** 📖 To... or the **Cc button** 📖 Cc...
☐ In the Subject text box, type the subject of the message
☐ In the message body, type the message
☐ Click the **Send button** 🖃 on the Standard toolbar

Button Method

☐ Click the **New list arrow** 🖃 on the Standard toolbar, then click **Mail Message**
☐ Follow the steps in the second through fifth bullets in the Compose and Send Messages Menu Method above

Keyboard Method

☐ Press **[Ctrl][Shift][M]**
☐ Follow the steps in the second through fifth bullets in the Compose and Send Messages Menu Method above

Respond to Messages

Menu Method

☐ Open and maximize the mail message to which you want to respond
☐ Click **Actions** on the menu bar, then click the appropriate option using Table OL-3 as a reference
☐ Type the message in the message body, then add any additional recipients as approrpriate
☐ Click the **Send button** 🖃 on the Standard toolbar

Button Method

☐ Open and maximize the mail message to which you want to respond
☐ Click the appropriate button on the Standard toolbar, using Table OL-3 as a reference
☐ Follow the steps in the third and fourth bullets in the Respond to Messages Menu Method above

Keyboard Method

☐ Open and maximize the mail message to which you want to respond
☐ Press the appropriate keyboard combination, using Table OL-3 as a reference
☐ Follow the steps in the third and fourth bullets in the Respond to Messages Menu Method above

Table OL-3 Message Response Options

Command on the Action menu	Button	Keyboard combination	Effect
Reply	[icon]	[Ctrl][R]	To send a message that includes the original text and your comments directly to the original sender
Reply to All	[icon]	[Ctrl][Shift][R]	To send a message that includes the original text and your comments directly to everyone on the original recipients' list
Forward	[icon]	[Ctrl][F]	To send a message that includes the original text and your comments directly to the recipient(s) of your choosing, but not to the sender

Create Office Documents From Within Outlook

Menu Method

☐ Click **File** on the menu bar, point to **New**, then click **Office Document**
☐ In the New Office Document dialog box, click the appropriate document type, then click **OK**
☐ When the program window opens, create the document as appropriate

Button Method

☐ Click the **New list arrow** [icon] on the Standard toolbar, then click **Office Document**
☐ Follow the second and third bullets in the Create Office Documents From Within Outlook Menu Method above

Keyboard Method

☐ Press **[Ctr][Shift][H]**
☐ Follow the second and third bullets in the Create Office Documents From Within Outlook Menu Method above

---

INSERT SIGNATURES AND ATTACHMENTS

Create Signatures

Menu Method

☐ Click **Tools** on the menu bar, then click **Options**
☐ In the Options dialog box, click the **Mail Format tab**
☐ Under Signature, click **Signatures**
☐ In the Create Signature dialog box, click **New**
☐ In the Create New Signature dialog box, type the signature name, select the appropriate option under Choose how to create your signature, then click **Next**

☐ In the Edit Signature dialog box, type the signature text, select any other appropriate options, then click **Finish**
☐ In the Signature dialog box, click **OK**, then click **OK** in the Create Signature dialog box
☐ Click **Apply** in the Options dialog box, then click **OK**

Insert Message Attachments

Menu Method

☐ Open a new message, then maximize the Untitled Message window
☐ Click **Insert** on the menu bar, then click **File**
☐ In the Insert File dialog box, navigate to the appropriate drive and folder, click the file, then click **Insert**

Button Method

☐ Open a new message, then maximize the Untitled Message window
☐ Click the **Insert File button** on the Standard toolbar
☐ In the Insert File dialog box, navigate to the appropriate drive and folder, click the file, then click **Insert**

CUSTOMIZE VIEWS

Menu Method

☐ Display the window (i.e. the Inbox window, the Notes window, the Calandar window, the Contacts folder, the Tasks window, or the Notes window) you want to customize
☐ Click **View** on the menu bar, point to **Current View**, then click **Customize Current View**
☐ In the View Summary dialog box, click the appropriate button using Table OL-4 as a reference, then click **OK**
☐ Click **OK** in the View Summary dialog box

Table OL-4 View Summary Dialog Box Options

Click this Button...	To open this dialog box...	To do...
Fields	Show Fields	Select fields to add, create a new field, or choose the order of the displayed fields
Group By	Group By	Select the order by which to group items, and whether to group in ascending or descending order
Sort	Sort	Select the items by which to sort, and whether to sort ascending or descending order
Filter	Filter	Select filter options such as search for a certain word or words, by sender, by time, by importance, whether there is an attachment, by message size, or by advanced options
Other Settings	Other Settings	Select fonts and size for the columns, and fonts for the row headers
Automatic Formatting	Automatic Formatting	Select rules (guidelines) and assign properties for the view

OUTLOOK SKILL SET 2: SCHEDULING

ADD APPOINTMENTS, MEETINGS, AND EVENTS TO THE OUTLOOK CALENDAR

Add Appointments to the Calendar

Menu Method

☐ Click **File** on the menu bar, point to **New**, then click **Appointment**
☐ In the Untitled – Appointment window, click the **Maximize button**, click the **Appointment tab** if necessary, then enter the subject, location, start and end time, and other appropriate information
☐ Click any other appropriate options, then click the **Save and Close button** 🖫 on the Standard toolbar

Button Method

☐ Click the **New list arrow** 🔽 on the Standard toolbar, then click **Appointment**
☐ Follow the steps in the second and third bullets in the Add Appointments to the Calendar Menu Method above

Keyboard Method

☐ Press **[Ctrl][Shift][A]**
☐ Follow the steps in the second and third bullets in the Add Appointments to the Calendar Menu Method above

Schedule Meetings and Invite Attendees

Menu Method

☐ Click **File** on the menu bar, point to **New**, then click **Meeting Request**
☐ In the Untitled - Meeting window, click the **Maximize button**, then click the **Appointment tab** if necessary
☐ Click the **To text box**, then enter recipient names or type the e-mail addresses, separating each with a semicolon (;), or to select recipient names from the Address Book, click the **To button** [To,..], then in the Select Attendees and Resources dialog box select the attendees and resources from the Name list box, click the appropriate button for each name (Required, Optional, Resources), then click **OK**
☐ Enter the subject, location, start and end time, and other appropriate information, then click the **Send button** 🔽 on the Standard toolbar

Button Method

☐ Click the **New list arrow** 🔽 on the Standard toolbar, then click **Meeting Request**
☐ Follow the steps in the second through fourth bullets in the Schedule Meetings and Invite Attendees Menu Method above

Keyboard Method

☐ Press **[Ctrl][Shift][Q]**
☐ Follow the steps in the second through fourth bullets in the Schedule Meetings and Invite Attendees Menu Method above

Schedule Resources for Meetings

Menu Method

Note: In order to schedule a resource, the resource must have its own mailbox and be included in your Contacts folder.

- [ ] In the Calendar window, click **Actions** on the menu bar, then click **Plan a Meeting**
- [ ] In the Plan a Meeting dialog box, click **Add Others**, then click **Add from Address Book**
- [ ] In the Select Attendees and Resources dialog box, enter the name of a resource you want at the meeting in the Type Name or Select from List text box, or click the name of the resource in the Name list box, then click **Resources**
- [ ] Repeat the previous bullet for each resource, then click **OK**
- [ ] Click **Make Meeting**
- [ ] In the Untitled – Meeting dialog box, click the **Maximize button**, enter the appropriate information, then click the **Send button** ⬛Send on the Standard toolbar
- [ ] Click **Close** to close the Plan a Meeting dialog box

APPLY CONDITIONAL FORMATS TO THE OUTLOOK CALENDAR

Menu Method

- [ ] In the Calendar window, click **View** on the menu bar, point to **Current View**, then click **Customize Current View**
- [ ] In the View Summary dialog box, click **Automatic Formatting**
- [ ] In the Automatic Formatting dialog box, click **Add**
- [ ] Type the condition name in the Name text box
- [ ] Click the **Label list arrow**, then click the appropriate label option
- [ ] Click **Condition**, specify the conditions in the Filter dialog box using Table OL-5 as a reference, then click **OK**
- [ ] Click **OK** in the Automatic Formatting dialog box, then click **OK** in the View Summary dialog box

Button Method

- [ ] In the Calendar window, click the **Calendar Coloring button** 🗓 on the Standard toolbar, then click **Automatic Formatting**
- [ ] Follow the steps in the third through seventh bullets in the Apply Conditional Formats to Appointments in the Calendar Menu Method above

Table OL-5 Filter Dialog Box Tabs

Tab	Options
Appointments and Meetings	Select filter options such as search for a certain word or words, by sender, or by time
More Choices	Select additional filter options such as by category or importance, whether there is an attachment, or by message size
Advanced	Define and add new advanced filter criteria

RESPOND TO MEETING REQUESTS

Accept and Decline Meeting Requests

Button Method

☐ In the Inbox window, open the meeting request to which you want to respond, then maximize the Meeting Request window
☐ Click the appropriate button on the Standard toolbar, using Table OL-6 as a reference
☐ In the message box, click the appropriate response option, then click **OK**

Table OL-6 Meeting Request Options

Button	Function
Accept button ✓	To accept the meeting at the proposed time and add it to your calendar
Tentative button ?	To tentatively accept the meeting and add it to your calendar
Decline button ✕	To decline the meeting and move the request to your

Propose New Meeting Times

Button Method

☐ In the Inbox, open the meeting request to which you want to respond, then maximize the Meeting Request window
☐ Click the **Propose New Time button** ▨ on the Standard toolbar
☐ In the Propose New time dialog box, select a new time, then click **Propose Time**
☐ In the New Time Proposed message window, type a note if necessary, then click the **Send button** ▨ on the Standard toolbar

USE CATEGORIES TO MANAGE APPOINTMENTS

Menu Method

- ☐ In the Calendar window, select the appropriate appointment(s)
- ☐ Click **Edit** on the menu bar, then click **Categories**, or right-click the appointment, then click **Categories** on the shortcut menu
- ☐ In the Categories dialog box, click the appropriate categories in the Available categories list box, then click **OK**

Button Method

- ☐ In the Calendar window, select the appropriate appointment(s)
- ☐ Click the **Organize button** 🗐 on the Standard toolbar
- ☐ In the Ways to Organize Calendar pane, click **Using Categories**
- ☐ Click the **Add appointments selected below to list arrow**, click the appropriate category, then click **Add**

PRINT CALENDARS

Print the Calendar in Two or More Views

Menu Method

- ☐ In the Calendar window, click **File** on the menu bar, then click **Print**
- ☐ In the Print dialog box, under Print style, click the option you want to print using Table OL-7 as an example, then click **OK**

Table OL-7 Print Style Options

Print Style	Preview
Daily	📰
Weekly	🗐
Monthly	▦
Tri-Fold	▥
Calendar Details	▦
Memo	📄

OUTLOOK SKILL SET 3: MANAGING MESSAGES

MOVE MESSAGES

Move Messages Between Folders

Menu Method
- ☐ In the Inbox window, click the appropriate message(s)
- ☐ Click **Edit** on the menu bar, then click **Move to Folder**
- ☐ In the Move Items dialog box, click the appropriate folder, then click **OK**

Button Method
- ☐ In the Inbox window, click the appropriate message(s)
- ☐ Click the **Move to Folder button** 🖼 on the Standard toolbar
- ☐ Click the appropriate folder on the menu, or click **Move to Folder**, then in the Move Items dialog box, click the appropriate folder, then click **OK**

Keyboard Method
- ☐ In the Inbox window, click the appropriate message(s)
- ☐ Press **[Ctrl][Shift][V]**
- ☐ In the Move Items dialog box, click the appropriate folder, then click **OK**

Mouse Method
- ☐ In the Inbox window, drag the message to the appropriate folder in the Folder List pane using ▧

Delete Messages

Menu Method
- ☐ In the Inbox window, click the appropriate message(s)
- ☐ Click **Edit** on the menu bar, then click **Delete**

Button Method
- ☐ In the Inbox window, click the appropriate message(s)
- ☐ Click the **Delete button** ☒ on the Standard toolbar

Keyboard Method
- ☐ In the Inbox window, click the appropriate message(s)
- ☐ Press **[Ctrl][D]** or **[Delete]**

SEARCH FOR MESSAGES

Menu Method
- ☐ In the Inbox window, click **Tools** on the menu bar, then click **Find**
- ☐ On the Find bar, type the search string in the Look for text box, type the location to search in the Search In text box, then click **Find Now**

Button Method
- ☐ In the Inbox window, click the **Find button** 🔍Find on the Standard toolbar
- ☐ On the Find bar, type the search string in the Look for text box, type the location to search in the Search In text box, then click **Find Now**

Keyboard Method

☐ In the Inbox window, press **[Ctrl][E]**
☐ On the Find bar, type the search string in the Look for text box, type the location to search in the Search In text box, then click **Find Now**

SAVE MESSAGES IN ALTERNATE FILE FORMATS

Menu Method

☐ In the Inbox window, click the message you want to save as a file, or open the message you want to save as a file, then maximize the message window
☐ Click **File** on the menu bar, then click **Save As**
☐ In the Save As dialog box, navigate to the appropriate drive and folder, then type a name for the file
☐ Click the **Save as type list arrow**, click the appropriate file format using Table OL-8 as a reference, then click **Save**

Table OL-8 Message File Formats

Option	Message can be opened in	Effect
Rich Text Format	Any text editor	Saves the text and formatting of a message to be opened and edited in a word processing program
Text Only	Any text editor	Saves the text of a message to be opened and edited in a word processing program, but does not save all formatting
Outlook Template	Microsoft Outlook	Can be used to create other messages
Message Format	Microsoft Outlook	Saves the message intact
HTML	A browser, such as Microsoft Internet Explorer	Can be displayed on the Web; the message must be created in HTML format in order to be saved as an HTML file

USE CATEGORIES TO MANAGE MESSAGES

Menu Method

☐ In the Inbox window, select the message(s)
☐ Click **Edit** on the menu bar, then click **Categories**, or right-click the message, then click **Categories** on the shortcut menu
☐ In the Categories dialog box, click the appropriate categories in the Available categories list box, then click **OK**

Set Message Options

Modify Message Settings

Button Method

☐ In the Inbox window, open and maximize a new message window
☐ Click the **Options button** 🔢 on the Standard toolbar
☐ In the Message Options dialog box, select the appropriate options, then click **Close**

Modify Delivery Options

Menu Method

☐ Click **Tools** on the menu bar, then click **Options**
☐ In the Options dialog box, click the **Mail Setup tab**
☐ Select the appropriate options, then click **OK**

Archive Messages Manually

Menu Method

☐ In the Inbox window, click **File** on the menu bar, then click **Archive**
☐ In the Archive dialog box, click the **Archive this folder and all subfolders option button**, then click the appropriate folder in the folders list
☐ Click any other appropriate options, then click **OK**

Outlook Skill Set 4: Creating and Managing Contacts

Create and Edit Contacts

Add Contacts

Menu Method

☐ Click **File** on the menu bar, point to **New**, then click **Contact**
☐ In the Untitled - Contact window, click the **Maximize button**, enter the name, address, phone number, e-mail, and other appropriate information
☐ Click the **Save and Close button** 🖫 on the Standard toolbar

Button Method

☐ Click the **New list arrow** 🔽 on the Standard toolbar, then click **Contact**
☐ Follow the steps in the second and third bullets in the Add Contacts Menu Method above

Keyboard Method

☐ Press **[Ctrl][Shift][C]**
☐ Follow the steps in the second and third bullets in the Add Contacts Menu Method above

Edit Contacts

Button Method

☐ In the Contacts window, double-click the contact to edit
☐ In the Contact window, click the **Maximize button**, make the appropriate modifications, then click the **Save and Close button** 🖫 on the Standard toolbar

Organize and Sort Contacts

Organize Contacts Using Categories

Menu Method

☐ In the Contacts window, select the contact(s)
☐ Click **Tools** on the menu bar, then click **Organize**
☐ In the Ways to Organize Contacts pane, click **Using Categories**
☐ Click the **Add contacts selected below to list arrow**, click the appropriate category, then click **Add**

Button Method

☐ In the Contacts window, select the contact(s)
☐ Click the **Organize button** 🔲 on the Standard toolbar
☐ Follow the third and fourth bullets in the Organize Contacts Using Categories Menu Method above

Sort Contacts

Menu Method

☐ In the Contacts window, click **View** on the menu bar, point to **Current View**, then click **Customize Current View**

☐ In the View Summary dialog box, click **Sort**

☐ In the Sort dialog box, select the appropriate sorting options, then click **OK**

☐ In the View Summary dialog box, click **OK**

LINK CONTACTS TO ACTIVITIES AND JOURNAL ENTRIES

Assign Categories to Contacts

Menu Method

☐ In the Contacts window, select the contact(s)

☐ Click **Edit** on the menu bar, then click **Categories**, or right-click the contact, then click **Categories** on the shortcut menu

☐ In the Categories dialog box, click the appropriate categories under the Available categories list, then click **OK**

Assign Journal Entries to Contacts

Menu Method

☐ Click **File** on the menu bar, point to **New**, then click **Journal Entry**

☐ In the Untitled – Journal Entry window, click the **Maximize button**, enter the subject, entry type, time, and other appropriate information, then click **Contacts**

☐ In the Select Contacts dialog box, select the contact(s) in the Items pane, then click **OK**

☐ Click the **Save and Close button** 🔲 on the Standard toolbar

Button Method

☐ Click the **New list arrow** 🔲 on the Standard toolbar, then click **Journal Entry**

☐ Follow the steps in the second through fourth bullets in the Assign Journal Entries to Contacts Menu Method above

Keyboard Method

☐ Press **[Ctrl][Shift][J]**

☐ Follow the steps in the second through fourth bullets in the Assign Journal Entries to Contacts Menu Method above

Tracking All Activities for Contacts

Button Method

☐ In the Contacts window, double-click the contact

☐ In the Contact window, click the **Maximize button**, then click the **Activities tab**

☐ Click the **Show list arrow**, then click the appropriate option

OUTLOOK SKILL SET 5: CREATING AND MANAGING TASKS AND NOTES

CREATE AND UPDATE TASKS

Create Tasks

Menu Method

- [ ] Click **File** on the menu bar, point to **New**, then click **Task**
- [ ] In the Untitled – Task window, click the **Maximize button**, then enter or select the appropriate information for the subject, dates, priority, reminders, and any other appropriate information
- [ ] Click the **Save and Close button** 🖫 on the Standard toolbar

Button Method

- [ ] Click the **New list arrow** 🖫 on the Standard toolbar, then click **Task**
- [ ] Follow the steps in the second and third bullets in the Create Tasks Menu Method above

Keyboard Method

- [ ] Press **[Ctrl][Shift][K]**
- [ ] Follow the steps in the second and third bullets in the Create Tasks Menu Method above

Update Tasks

Button Method

- [ ] In the Tasks window, open and maximize the appropriate task
- [ ] Make the appropriate modifications
- [ ] Click the **Save and Close button** 🖫 on the Standard toolbar

MODIFY TASK ORGANIZATION AND TASK VIEW

Assign Tasks to One or More Contacts

Menu Method

- [ ] Click **File** on the menu bar, point to **New**, then click **Task Request**
- [ ] In the Untitled – Task window, click the **Maximize button**, type each recipient's name in the To text box separated by a semi-colon, or click the **To button** To... , select the people in the Select Attendees and Resources dialog box, then click **TO**
- [ ] Repeat the previous bullet for each recipient, then click **OK**.
- [ ] Select any other appropriate options, then click the **Send button** 🖃 on the Standard toolbar

Button Method

- [ ] Click the **New list arrow** 🖫 on the Standard toolbar, then click **Task Request**
- [ ] Follow the steps in the second and third bullets in the Assign Tasks to One or More Contacts Menu Method above

Keyboard Method

☐ Press **[Ctrl][Shift][U]**
☐ Follow the steps in the second and third bullets in the Assign Tasks to One or More Contacts Menu Method above

ACCEPT, DECLINE, OR DELEGATE TASKS

Delegate Tasks

Menu Method

☐ In the Tasks window, open and maximize the appropriate task
☐ Click **Actions** on the menu bar, then click **Assign Task**
☐ Type each recipient's name in the To text box separated by a semi-colon, or click the **To button** To.. , select the people in the Select Task Receipient dialog box, then click **To**
☐ Repeat the previous bullet for each recipient, then click **OK**
☐ Select any other appropriate options, then click the **Send button** 📧 on the Standard toolbar
☐ If a message box regarding reminders appears, click **OK**

Button Method

☐ In the Tasks window, open and maximize the appropriate task
☐ Click the **Assign Task button** 📧 on the Standard toolbar
☐ Follow the steps in the third through sixth bullets in the Delegate Tasks Menu Method above

Accept and Decline Tasks

Button Method

☐ In the Tasks window, open and maximize the appropriate task
☐ Click the **Accept button** ✅ or the **Decline button** ❌ on the Standard toolbar as appropriate
☐ In the Accepting Tasks or the Declining Tasks dialog box, click the appropriate response option, then click **OK**
☐ If necessary, type the response in the message window
☐ Click the **Send button** 📧 on the Standard toolbar

CREATE AND MODIFY NOTES

Create Notes

Menu Method

☐ Click **File** on the menu bar, point to **New**, then click **Note**
☐ In the Note window, type the appropriate information
☐ Click the **Close button** ❌ on the Note window title bar

Button Method

☐ Click the **New list arrow** 📄 on the Standard toolbar, then click **Note**
☐ Follow the steps in the second and third bullets in the Create Notes Menu Method above

Keyboard Method

☐ Press **[Ctrl][Shift][N]**
☐ Follow the steps in the second and third bullets in the Create Notes Menu Method above

Edit Notes

Menu Method

☐ In the Notes window, select the appropriate note
☐ Click **File** on the menu bar, point to **Open**, then click **Selected Items**, or right-click the note, then click **Open** on the shortcut menu
☐ Make the edits to the note, then click the **Close button** ☒ on the Notes window title bar

Mouse Method

☐ In the Notes window, double-click the appropriate note
☐ Make the edits to the note, then click the **Close button** ☒ on the Notes window title bar

Forward a Note to a Contact

Menu Method

☐ In the Notes window, select the appropriate note
☐ Click **Actions** on the menu bar, then click **Forward**, or right-click the note, then click **Forward** on the shortcut menu
☐ In the Untitled - Message window, click the **Maximize button**, type the recipient name(s) or type the e-mail address in the To and Cc boxes, separating each name with a semicolon (;), or to select recipient names from the Address Book, click the **To button** 🔳 **To...** or the **Cc button** 🔳 **Cc...**
☐ In the Subject text box, type the subject of the message
☐ In the message body, type the message
☐ Click the **Send button** 🔳 on the Standard toolbar

Keyboard Method

☐ In the Notes window, select the appropriate note
☐ Press **[Ctrl][F]**
☐ Follow the steps in the third through sixth bullets in the Forward a Note to a Contact Menu Method above

---

USE CATEGORIES TO MANAGE TASKS AND NOTES

Menu Method

☐ In the Notes window or the Tasks window, select the note(s) or task(s)
☐ Click **Edit** on the menu bar, then click **Categories**, or right-click the note or task, then click **Categories** on the shortcut menu
☐ In the Categories dialog box, click the appropriate categories under the Available categories list, then click **OK**

INDEX